Dark Psychology & Manipulation 2 in 1:

How to Understand and Manipulate with Anyone, Overthinking, Persuasion, Recognise Someone Trying to Manipulate with You, Self Confidence, Best to Listen in Car

2 Books in 1

Dark Psychology..........................4

Manipulation............................119

© Copyright 2019 Tony Bennis - All rights reserved.

The following eBook is reproduced below with the goal of providing information that is as accurate and reliable as possible. Regardless, purchasing this eBook can be seen as consent to the fact that both the publisher and the author of this book are in no way experts on the topics discussed within and that any recommendations or suggestions that are made herein are for entertainment purposes only. Professionals should be consulted as needed prior to undertaking any of the action endorsed herein.

This declaration is deemed fair and valid by both the American Bar Association and the Committee of Publishers Association and is legally binding throughout the United States.

Furthermore, the transmission, duplication, or reproduction of any of the following work including specific information will be considered an illegal act irrespective of if it is done electronically or in print. This extends to creating a secondary or tertiary copy of the work or a recorded copy and is only allowed with an expressed written consent from the Publisher. All additional rights reserved.

The information in the following pages is broadly considered to be a truthful and accurate account of facts and as such any inattention, use, or misuse of the information in question by the reader will render any resulting actions solely under their purview. There are no scenarios in which the publisher or the original author of this work can be in any fashion deemed liable for any hardship or damages that may befall them after undertaking information described herein.

Additionally, the information in the following pages is intended only for informational purposes and should thus be thought of as universal. As befitting its nature, it is presented without assurance regarding its prolonged validity or interim quality. Trademarks that are mentioned are done without written consent and can in no way be considered an endorsement from the trademark holder.

Dark Psychology:

A Powerful Guide to Learn Persuasion, Psychological Warfare, Deception, Mind Control, Negotiation, NLP, Human Behavior and Manipulation! Great to Listen in a Car!

Table of contents

Introduction..8

Chapter one: The principles of dark psychology......10

Chapter two: "Dark personality" traits....................18

Chapter three: Studies of dark psychology..............36

Chapter four: Mind reading....................................47

Chapter five: Cognitive psychology........................64

Chapter six: Modes of persuasion..........................83

Chapter seven: Controlling emotions.....................98

Chapter eight: Social engineering and leadership..108

Conclusion..118

© Copyright 2019 Tony Bennis - All rights reserved.

The following eBook is reproduced below with the goal of providing information that is as accurate and reliable as possible. Regardless, purchasing this eBook can be seen as consent to the fact that both the publisher and the author of this book are in no way experts on the topics discussed within and that any recommendations or suggestions that are made herein are for entertainment purposes only. Professionals should be consulted as needed prior to undertaking any of the action endorsed herein.

This declaration is deemed fair and valid by both the American Bar Association and the Committee of Publishers Association and is legally binding throughout the United States.

Furthermore, the transmission, duplication, or reproduction of any of the following work including specific information will be considered an illegal act irrespective of if it is done electronically or in print. This extends to creating a secondary or tertiary copy of the work or a recorded copy and is only allowed with an expressed written consent from the Publisher. All additional rights reserved.

The information in the following pages is broadly considered to be a truthful and accurate account of facts and as such any inattention, use, or misuse of the information in question by the reader will render any resulting actions solely under their purview. There are no scenarios in which the publisher or the original author of this work can be in any fashion deemed liable for any hardship or damages that may befall them after undertaking information described herein.

Additionally, the information in the following pages is intended only for informational purposes and should thus be thought of as universal. As befitting its nature, it is presented without assurance regarding its prolonged validity or interim quality. Trademarks that are mentioned are done without written consent and can in no way be considered an endorsement from the trademark holder

Introduction

Congratulations on and thank you for downloading Dark Psychology. Here we will explore the more sordid and dark aspects of the human psyche, as well as some methods of applying our knowledge for use in our everyday lives. Here the following areas will be delved into the principles of dark psychology, "dark personality" traits, studies of dark psychology, mind reading, cognitive psychology, modes of persuasion, controlling emotions, and social engineering and leadership.

This book DOES NOT offer any formal health benefits and is intended for educational purposes only. Any health benefits or detriments associated with reading this book are merely circumstantial and coincidental. The writer does not condone using any information expressed here to better one's health.

Dark psychology accepts and embraces the darker side of the human experience. In this way it is doing the same as any area of anthropocentric study does, the only difference lying in dark psychology's specialty of this dark reality within the human animal. Dark psychology is not meant to be a pageant of villains, however. Specialists within this field do their work in order to better understand why and how malevolent people work toward their ends, not out of some attempt to gain fame for themselves and or to idolize the more monstrous among us. It is also important to keep in mind that each and every one of us has a dark or "evil" side of our own psychology. While there are some other conduits by which we can reach the realization of this side's contents, it is dark psychology that provides the clearest route for us in our way toward our enlightenment concerning how dark we truly are and why.

As you can tell, we have a lot of ground to cover within this book, so we should now dive on into our first subject regarding dark psychology: its principles.

Chapter one: The principles of dark psychology

Dark psychology could best be described as a study of the human condition in which it becomes normative for people to pray upon others out of criminal and or deviant desires. Often these desires lack specific purpose and are based primarily on basic instinctual desires. Each human has the potential and capacity to victimize other humans, as well as other living creatures, but most of us keep these desires suppressed in order to function successfully in society. Those of us who do not sublimate these dark tendencies are typically representative of the "dark triad": psychopathy, sociopathy, and Machiavellianism, or other mental disorders/psychological disturbances. In this way, dark psychology focuses primarily on the underpinnings (i.e. the thoughts, processing systems, feelings, and behaviors) that are found below the more predatory aspects of our nature, the same ones that go most vigorously against the grain of modern thought concerning human behavior. In this field, we tend to assume that these more abusive, criminal, and deviant behaviors are purposive most of the time, though there are instances in which they seem to have no teleological underpinnings.

Dark psychology accepts and embraces the darker side of the human experience. In this way it is doing the same as any area of anthropocentric study does, the only difference lying in dark psychology's specialty of this dark reality within the human animal. Dark psychology is not meant to be a pageant of villains, however. Specialists within this field do their work in order to better understand why and how malevolent people work toward their ends, not out of some attempt to gain fame for themselves and or to idolize the more monstrous among us. It is also important to keep in mind that each and every one of us has a dark or "evil" side of our own psychology. While there are some other conduits by which we can reach the realization of this side's contents, it is dark psychology that provides the clearest route for us in our way toward our enlightenment concerning how dark we truly are and why.

Wrongdoing, as Socrates asserts, is doing that harms others. Not only does this harm others, but Socrates also thought that it harms our own souls, as many modern people would agree. Dark psychologists allow that some of us do wrong onto others for no greater purposes. Their ends never justify their means because there are simply no ends to be found. This capability (and perhaps even proclivity) for harm within cause or purposiveness can be found within all of us. The field of dark psychology assumes justifiably that these irrational desires to harm within us are incredibly complex and harm to understand.

Whether wrongdoing is purposive or even intentional, and whether it is done out of want of money, retaliation, or power, the most destructive force behind wrongdoing is aggression. Aggression is likely the single biggest adversary of prosocial relations, and it should not be confused with assertiveness. Aggression is any verbal and or physical behavior that is meant to harm or destroy. This aim is what differentiates it from other classes of behaviors that bring harm or destruction with no aims.

Biologically, there are certain genetic markers that are more indicative of aggression than others. Neurologically, it is the amygdala that controls most aggressive behavioral patterns. For this reason, people with enlarged and deformed amygdala typically commit violent acts at higher rates. As far as hormones are concerned, it is usually those people (primarily young men) with higher levels of testosterone and lower levels of serotonin who tend to be the most violent. The most aggressive people within societies are typically ones who have been put through something of a loop: their testosterone levels rise and cause them to become aggressive, which in turn begets higher levels of testosterone and even more aggression. In this way, some of the most dangerous people the world has to offer are created. Drugs and foods that increase serotonin and decrease testosterone levels are typically the best options for decreasing overall levels of aggression.

The most common cause of aggression is a failure or being stopped short of a goal. Studies indicate that those who have been made miserable by such unfortunate events usually make others around them more miserable as well. In these unpleasant instances, we naturally become frustrated, which begets our being angered, and once we are angered we can easily become aggressive if given a cue. Some of the most common stimuli that can cue aggressive behaviors are personal insults (perhaps the most common), cigarette smoke, foul odors, and hot temperatures. Ostracism is another common cause of aggression, causing some of the same neurological phenomena as physical pain does.

One of the most tragic causes of increased aggression is the knowledge that aggression can be rewarding in some instances. Children who learn early that aggression can pay out (so to speak) are much more likely to remain aggressive throughout life. Other social influences that can cause higher rates of aggression include the absence of one or both parents during the formative years, with the father figure usually being the one absent. In order to stop aggressive behavior before it starts, despite the family conditions, the best possible model to instill is one that rewards cooperation and sensitivity from an early age. Parents and caregivers should be models for these modes of conduct, but exasperated parents who do not have effective systems in place tend to become brash and even aggressive themselves with their children, often creating intergenerational lineages of aggression with their actions.

One of, if not the most, troubling aspects of human nature is sexual aggression. Rapes are typically committed by males against women. These have multifarious causes but are often of a mixture of sexual promiscuity (or the impersonal approach to sex) combined with hostile and aggressive masculinity.

In addition to the amygdala, the midbrain and the hypothalamus are also central in aggression, in all mammals. The hypothalamus has specialized receptors that determine levels of aggression based on the levels of serotonin and vasopressin that they are exposed to. Midbrain areas that deal with aggression have connections to both the brainstem and others structures such as the prefrontal cortex and the amygdala. Stimulation of the amygdala typically leads to higher levels of aggression within mammals, while lesions on this area (or on the hippocampus) typically lead to a reduction of the expression of social dominance out of the regulation of aggression and or fear.

The prefrontal cortex is an area crucial to the regulation of self-control and the inhibition of impulses, specifically aggressive ones. A reduction in the prefrontal cortex, particularly in its orbitofrontal and medial portions, is positively correlated with higher levels of violent and antisocial aggression. Response inhibition is also found to be lower in most violent offenders.

Again, a deficiency in serotonin levels is one of the most common causes of aggression and impulsivity. Lower levels of serotonin transmission can affect other neurochemical systems, including the dopamine system, which regulates motivation towards results and attention levels. Norepinephrine also influences levels of overall aggression, working within the hormonal system, the sympathetic nervous system, and the central nervous system. The neuropeptides oxytocin and vasopressin also play large roles in the regulation of social recognition, attachment, and aggression within mammals. Oxytocin plays its most important role in the regulation of female bonds with mates and offspring, as well as the use of protective and retaliatory aggression. Vasopressin is more so used for the regulation of aggression in males.

When we think of dark psychology one of the most common terms that comes to mind is "predator". Human predators come in all shapes and sizes and work to various means, but all of them have one thing in common if they are successful: persuasion. Predators of all types know who to "strum the strings that are inside all of us" as social psychologist Robert Cialdini puts it. These are people who look for attunement from all those who they come across, or the compliance to their own authority, whether it be real or imaginary.

The first thing that predators seek to establish over others is authority. They tend to look for the things that other people most desire, and then offer these things under the (usually false) guise of authority figures. They project confidence when around people who they think that they can influence. If they are well spoken then they usually are more successful in this practice, as we tend to question those who we find more well-spoken much less. One of the most fitting adjectives that could be used to describe most predators is impotence. These are typically people who have felt little to no power in their lives, being constantly subjected to the wills of others and never feeling that same sense of authority themselves, they start to seek our victims who they perceive as weaker than they are.

Another way in which predators operate to their ends is by fostering a sense of reciprocity within their victims. They will usually lure their victims in with gifts and or favors, only to trap them later with obligations to be fulfilled in order to pay back debts. These gifts and favors not only force victims to spend more time around their perpetrators but also divert their attention from the true aims of the predators. It is through this labyrinth of debts labors that victims can spend months to even years and decades of their lives in unnecessary contact with predatory people.

Similarity between people is one of the most common causes of liking. What more, once we have decided that we like another person we become much more likely to do things, things that they ask of us. This is why predators use many different ways to increase rapport with their victims, including the use of compliments, common identity, and common interests to trap their victims. In this way malevolent people can harm others without even being detected, only being perceived as friends and allies by their unwitting victims. Most predators are surprising to common people in that they are able to put on likable personas for themselves just as well as more benevolent people. They typically know how to imitate "normal" people with ease and seamlessness that allows them to work towards their malevolent ends without being detected by people with no expertise in the area of predation. Most are endowed with the same sense of conformity that we all are, but this conformity does not always apply to their actions as they manipulate their way through life.

Predators are always looking for what it is that potential victims want. Successful ones are able to easily tell what presses other people's buttons, and what it is that others most desire. Once they have ascertained what bait they should use to get what they want, they step in to provide the social proof to the victim that asserts that they are in the right and that they have everything that the victim is looking for. These are people who can almost smell our desires and insecurities, and who are ready and able to get the more gullible of us to do their bidding.

Since predators rely heavily on the power of commitment within their victims, they tend to seek out only people who they think will feel the most indebted to them. Initially, a predatory figure will elicit smaller commitments from their victims, which usually only lead into larger and larger ones as time goes on. When others let them, predators tend to pile on these commitments until it becomes difficult to disengage with them. This is usually when the darker side of the predator shows itself, and those who are in contact with him or her start to feel disillusioned.

If we want to avoid the predation of others, we have to introspect on our own vulnerabilities, as these are exactly the things that malevolent people are going to look for within us. We should also introspect on our own predatory behaviors as well, as none of us are immune to malevolence. Each one of us is both predatory and submissive, so reconciling these two selves is essential to better understanding ourselves and others.

Chapter two: "Dark personality" traits

We tend to focus all too much on the lighter side of human psychology. Whether followers of the "positive psychology" movement or not, we often have difficulty seeing the value in the more rank underbelly of human psychology, the dark side. This happens to our detriment though, as it is the more bothersome aspects of our nature that tend to enlighten us more than the personas that people put on. Here we will delve into the darker traits of human psychology, the ones that all contain one overarching trait more destructive than any others: callousness or a lack of empathy for others. Those who have these traits are very diverse, but they all share the potential to harm others due to their inability to empathize.

The first of these traits, and perhaps the most common is narcissism. We all display this negative trait at one point or another, so it is usually best to reserve judgment when others come across as narcissistic upon first glance. Narcissists often disregard the thoughts and feelings of others and take advantage of people in order to get what they want. Witnessing other people getting attention and admiration frustrates them, as they believe that they are entitled to these things above others. This trait, like any other, exists on a spectrum within people, with the most pretentious of us at the top and the ones with least self-efficacy at the bottom.

Although all of us experience narcissistic traits in varying degrees, in around 1% of the population these traits can take on a more severe, pathological form in which the person gains an unrealistic perception of his or her own abilities and is in constant need of attention and admiration. This pathologized form of narcissism is called narcissistic personality disorder.

Narcissistic supply is a sort of admiration, sustenance, or interpersonal support drawn by a narcissist out of his or her environment. This supply can easily become essential to the maintenance of the narcissist's self-esteem if it is never kept from him or her. For this reason, narcissists tend to seek out those who will admire them irrationally and there is very little that will stop a narcissist once he or she has found some sort of relationship in which there are unjustified resources allocated interpersonally. This need for the admiration or attention of codependents is considered pathological because it does not take into account the feeling, thoughts, and or needs of the other people involved. The narcissist only considers his or her supply and is never focused on what is actually going on with those other people involved.

Narcissistic injury is a perceived threat to the narcissist's self-esteem. Other terms interchangeable with this one are narcissistic blow, narcissistic scar, and narcissistic wound. What all of these have in common, however, is what they are met with narcissistic rage. Narcissistic rage is a common reaction to any form of narcissistic injury. This rage (like any other sort of rage) exists within a continuum, ranging from mild remoteness to harsher expressions of annoyance and frustration, and finally to intense emotional outbursts, sometimes including violent attacks.

Narcissistic rage can manifest itself in many other ways as well. These include depressive, paranoid delusion, and catatonic episodes. It is also widely held that most narcissists have two main types of rage. The first of these types is rage constantly directed at one or more other people, while the second type is constantly directed at the self. Narcissistic rage is not necessarily troublesome in its severity, as its severity exists on a similar spectrum as does "normal" rage, but becomes more problematic when considering that it is inherently pathological.

A narcissistic defense is any process whereby the idealized self portrait of the narcissist is preserved, while any of its actual limitations are denied. In other words, this type of defense is found when the narcissist is trying to preserve his or her own self image more so than trying to ascertain the truth about the self. These defenses tend to be very rigid, as the narcissist anchors as much as possible to the most self flattering narratives imaginable. Most narcissists actually do experience feelings of guilt or shame (both conscious and unconscious) quite often, and one of the most common methods by which they alleviate these negative feelings is by putting up such defenses. Pathological narcissism has to find psychological shortcuts in order to survive throughout greater self-realization, and narcissistic defense is likely the most common of these shortcuts.

The original definition of narcissistic abuse referred more to the abuse committed by narcissistic parents on their children. Typically, this type of abuse consists of the children of narcissists having to give up parts of their own feelings and wants in order to protect their parents' self-esteems. Children who grow up being subjected to this type of abuse often have codependency issues later on in life. Having no knowledge of what constitutes a normal relationship, they tend to be unable to recognize who it is who they will be better off with and who to avoid. It is common that they will formulate further relationships with more narcissists who have similar pathologies to those of their parents.

In more recent years this term has been more widely applied to abuse within relationships among adults. Adult narcissists are about as likely to abuse other adults as they are to abuse children. These abusive relationships typically do not last as long due to the fact that adult victims usually have much more mobility to get out of the relationships than do child victims.

The next dark trait is Machiavellianism. This term can be applied to both the political philosophy of Niccolò Machiavelli and a manipulative personality trait. Here only the later usage will apply. This trait is most commonly characterized by a deceitful personality style, a pathological focus on personal gain and self-interest, an overall deficiency of empathy, and a blatant disregard for morality.

One of the most troubling aspects of Machiavellians is their overall lack of emotion. This often leads them to be influenced very little by "conventional" modes of morality and to subsequently manipulate and deceive others without remorse in order to meet their own personal needs. This trait is measured in units called machs by psychologists. People with higher levels of machs are shown to agree more with statements such as "never tell others your reasoning unless it benefits you to do so", and less with statements such as "people are generally good", "there is never an excuse to lie to others", or "the most successful among us lead moral lives". Typically, males score higher levels of machs than do females.

Machiavellians are typically rather cold and selfish people who see others mostly as instruments they can use to serve their own interests. The motives that they have in mind at any given point in time, whether they be sexual, social, professional, etc., are often pursued in duplicitous manners, with little to no thought of the wellbeing of the other parties involved in mind. Those with higher levels of machs tend to be motivated more by power, money, and competition than anything else, while those with lower levels of machs tend to focus more on things such as family commitment, self-love, and community building. People with higher levels of machs want to win at any cost, no matter how steep. With these views in mind, we could reasonably argue that people who are more Machiavellian than others are also more bent toward avarice. These people are typically much less motivated by altruistic sentiments and any forms of philanthropy, and instead, spend most of their time in aimless competition and malevolent industry. For these reasons, Machiavellians are usually much less trustworthy and much more self-interested than others.

It is only their outstanding abilities in manipulating others that give Machiavellians the reputation of being an intelligent group of people. In reality, there is no verifiable correlation between machs and IQ scores, but the stereotype of the intelligent Machiavellian shifting his or her way through vast webs of action and coming out with everything in mind persists, nevertheless. Emotional intelligence is, however, not a strong point of most Machiavellians. Higher levels of machs are typically correlated with lower EQ scores. Both emotional recognition and emotional empathy are negatively correlated with Machiavellianism. This trait has also never been shown to be correlated to a more advanced theory of mind. This suggests that Machiavellians are not necessarily better able to understand what others are thinking in social situations, so any abilities in manipulation they might possess are not related to their theory of mind.

Among some psychological circles, Machiavellianism is considered to be merely a subclinical form of psychopathy.

While this personality trait is closely related to psychopathy and overlaps with it in several areas of thought, most psychologists hold that it is, in fact, an entirely independent personality construct. Psychopaths are generally much more impulsive and have less self-control than Machiavellians. Both of these traits do share dishonesty, however. Machiavellians are also typically much less agreeable and conscientious than the general population, which often leads to their finding little success in their careers and personal relationships. Machiavellians are also high in agency and low in communion, meaning that they seek to individuate and succeed more than they seek work with others in communal efforts. This is not necessarily a bad combination of traits in of itself, but what is troubling about many Machiavellians is that they often desire not only to succeed themselves but also seek actively to do so at the expense of others.

What makes many Machiavellians so effective in what they do is their ability to stay under people's radars. There are, however, some fundamental ways in which we can clearly identify these dangerous people before they start to wreak havoc on our lives.

One of the greatest indicators of truly high machs in a person is that person's ability to function especially well in workplaces and other social situations in which the rules are ambiguous. With no clear cut boundaries, these people are going to inevitably roam in every direction they see fit, and will constantly be thinking of ways to advance their own interests at the costs of the company that they keep. Machiavellians thrive most where lines are blurred and all behaviors seem unprecedented, because where these vulnerable settings exist they see opportunities to take actions that they will not be held responsible for.

Another red flag is excessive emotional detachment, sometimes coupled with a cynical outlook on things that enables the person to wait patiently and passionlessly for any opportunities that might present themselves. With this impulse control, Machiavellians are better able to plan ahead and to determine what they can do to manipulate than others are.

Machiavellians are also characterized by their use of pressure, guilt, self-disclosure, charm, and politeness in order to meet their ends. These tactics allow them to maneuver socially toward their malevolent goals without being detected. In addition to using these tactics, they also prepare backup plans to cut themselves out of corners when they are caught. Endless excuses and diversions are often employed when they are outed, the multiplicity of which can be overwhelming to those who do try to expose them.

The true potency of Machiavellianism lies within its covertness. These people are able to manipulate others so effectively because, in part, no one suspects them of harboring ulterior motives in the things that they do. Under the guise of normal, benevolent people they are often able to blend seamlessly into the foliage of wholesome citizenry.

Psychopathy is perhaps the most well-known and disturbing of the dark traits. Psychopathy as a personality disorder is characterized by ongoing antisocial behaviors, impaired capacity to empathize, and certain egotistical, disinhibited, and bold traits.

There are two mains types of psychopathy, characterized by their symptoms. The first (and less problematic) type is known as Cleckleyan psychopathy, characterized by disinhibited and bold behavioral patterns. The second type is criminal psychopathy, characterized by more aggressive and disinhibited behaviors, in this case, criminal. Of these two types, the latter is obviously more paid attention to due to the fact that a large portion of the world's most notorious criminals have suffered from this type of psychopathy.

The first of the psychopathic traits is often the one that allows all others to become unmanageable: boldness. This trait is constituted by a low level of fear combined with a high stress tolerance, a general toleration of danger and uncertainty, and incredibly high levels of assertiveness and self-confidence. An excess of this trait may or may not be related to individual variations of the amygdala, the brain's most important regulator of fear. With this boldness psychopaths are often able to handle people and situations that normal people would much rather shy away from. This can work the advantage of the psychopath but does often get him or her into more trouble than is necessary. With this trait, psychopaths often have a hard time distinguishing actual threats from normal occurrences, because their neural circuitry is simply not indicating to them that things are one way or the other.

Disinhibition is the next trait of psychopaths. This term refers to a lack of impulse control combined with issues concerning planning, a lack of control over urges, a constant need to instant gratification, and an overall poor restraints on behavior. This trait in excess often corresponds with impairments in structures within the frontal lobe that influences these types of behavioral control systems. Disinhibition causes many psychopaths to act impulsively and even erratically when following their immediate desires. Always living for the moment, they never have a clear sight of what might happen next or what they should do to give themselves lasting gratification. This often leads them to make worse decisions which damage them more because so many of the things that give us instant gratification end up harming us greatly in the long run.

Another common trait of psychopaths is that of meanness or cruelty. Psychopaths often lack empathy and have little to no intimate relationships with others, sometimes even being disdainful of the company of others. They often use cruelty in order to obtain greater power, are generally much more exploitative than others, recalcitrant towards authority figures, and tend to seek out excitement in careless and dangerous fashions. This trait is likely more destructive to those who come into contact with psychopaths than any of the others mentioned here. Psychopaths typically do not enjoy the company of others, so when they are around others they are all the more likely to act in cruel and callous manners because they perceive that they have nothing to lose. This outlook on others causes them to act in ways that are disagreeable and sometimes dangerous, whether with a purposiveness for doing so in mind or not.

Typically, psychopaths are rather high in antagonism, and very low in conscientiousness and in anxiety, feeling almost no anxiety, in fact. These people are also low in socialization and responsibility and high in sensation seeking, impulsivity, and aggression. The combination of these traits tend to create people who do not get along with others well, who contribute little product to society at large, and who follow their impulses freely and without anxiety.

Of the other dark personality traits, psychopathy is probably most closely related to narcissism. One psychological perspective, in fact, even considers this trait as just another part of the pathological narcissism spectrum. Some psychologists assert that narcissistic personality exists on the bottom of this spectrum, malignant narcissism in the middle, and psychopathy at its highest point.

Socially, the main symptoms of psychopathy are callousness, manipulation, and sometimes crime and violence. Mentally, the impairment of processes related to cognition and affect are the biggest indicators of psychopathy. These symptoms usually start to come about around adolescence, though they are sometimes found even in younger children and are at other times not found until later in adulthood.

Psychopathy scores are surprisingly telltale concerning incarceration records. Higher scores of this trait are often found to be correlated with a repeated bout of imprisonment, holdings within higher security areas of detention centers, more disciplinary infractions, and higher rates of substance abuse.

While psychopathy is not entirely synonymous with violence, there are lots of well noted correlations between this trait and violent acts. Psychopathy is often characterized by "instrumental" aggression. This form of aggression is more proactive and or predatory than others are. Subdued emotion and goals not directed but largely facilitated by the causing of harm are two other characteristics of this potent form of aggression. Instrumental aggression is often correlated with homicide offenses because of the predatory nature of this form of aggression.

Psychopathy is also linked to domestic violence, with around 15-30% of perpetrators showing psychopathic tendencies. It is mainly the callousness, combined with the disdain of interpersonal connections, that causes many psychopaths to commit domestic violence offences. Despite all of these connections that psychopathy has with various types of violent criminal behavior, psychopathic tendencies are still not widely considered in risk assessment.

Sex crime is another gruesome sort of criminal activity that is commonly associated with psychopathy due to a psychopathic proclivity towards violent sexual behavior. The relationship between psychopathy and child molestation is shown in the number of offences by the perpetrator, which tends to rise in more psychopathic individuals. Tendencies towards sadistic violence and a lack or remorse tend to cause psychopaths to commit sex crimes that normal people would simply never imagine. Despite this disconcerting proclivity to reoffend, psychopaths are on average 2.5 times more likely to be granted conditional releases than are their non-psychopathic counterparts when imprisoned for their crimes.

Psychopathy is also correlated with organized crime, war crime, and economic crime. It is the antisocial violence, the worldview that precludes the welfare of others, the incessant externalization of blame, the lack of remorse, and the impulsivity that tends to drive psychopaths towards criminal behaviors of all kinds at higher rates than non-psychopaths. While terrorism is popularly associated with psychopathy, psychopaths are actually less likely to engage in terrorist activity because of the planning, organization, and frequent communal working that goes into staging terrorist attacks. Terrorism appeals less to psychopaths because of their own selfish intuitions as well.

In childhood and adolescence, the most common precursors of psychopathy are emotionlessness or callousness, impulsivity or responsibility, and narcissism. The trait and or personality disorder can be so difficult to discern or to diagnose within these early stages because its symptoms are found in so many non-psychopathic children and adolescents. These traits are, whether found in psychopaths or normal individuals, often indicative of later violent or criminal behavior. In juveniles, psychopathy is usually correlated with higher rates of negative emotions such as depression, anxiety, hostility, and anger. Although we may have certain indicators of psychopathy in younger people, these indicators usually to not manifest themselves into actual psychopathy later on in life and are typically individual issues instead.

Conduct disorder in juveniles is seen as a pathway to later antisocial personality disorder and psychopathy. This disorder usually stems from a toxic mixture of preexisting neurological issues and prolonged exposure to adverse environmental factors. Not only do those with this disorder display prolonged antisocial behaviors throughout life, but they are also shown to remain in poorer overall health and usually have much lower socio economic status. Childhood onset starts before 10 and typically results in more long term antisocial behavior, while adolescent onset starts after 10 and more often results in antisocial behavior limited to the short term.

It is when conduct disorder is intermixed with ADHD that the antisocial behaviors associated with it become their most problematic. Younger people with this combination of disorders tend to show the same callousness, aggression, and behavioral inhibition as psychopaths of all ages display. The remorseless and unemotional interpersonal style of those with conduct disorder is one of psychology's most remarkable parallels to psychopathy.

As far as mentality is concerned, dysfunctions within the amygdala and the prefrontal cortex are the most common neurological causes of psychopathy. These dysfunctions are often inborn, though they are at other times caused by tumors, legions, and traumatic brain injuries sustained by these regions. While patients with these issues in these regions may resemble in thought and action psychopaths, they are divorced from the latter group. Whether psychopathic or non-psychopathic, people with damage to the regions of the brain typically have a much more difficult time learning social and moral reasoning than most people do. Stimulus reinforced learning is also impaired within individuals with damage to these regions, meaning that whether being rewarded or punished, these people have difficulty learning based on what effects are stemming from what they are doing.

Despite these learning defects, there is no unassailable link between psychopathy and IQ. Regarding intelligence, psychopaths as a group are really a rather accurate reflection of the general population, with some being incredibly brilliant and some being very dull by contrast, while the majority is about average.

Psychopathy is also linked to unusual responses to distress cues. Vocal and physical responses to fear and sadness are often either looked over or misinterpreted by psychopaths usually because of a decrease in activity within the fusicore and extrastriate regions of the brain. This inactivity results in the failure to recognize all emotions on other people's faces as well, but it is the inability to discern fear and sadness that usually works most to the detriment of psychopaths.

Amorality is one of the more problematic byproducts of psychopathy. Here this term refers to a disregard for, an indifference towards, or just an absence of moral sentiments and practices. There are two main areas of concern within most moral reasoning: personal transgressions and compliance (or noncompliance) with conventional rules. Socrates noted these areas as the adherence of natural and conventional laws respectively. When asked to determine which types of these laws should be followed more closely, psychopaths generally assert that it is the conventional laws whereas non-psychopaths usually believe that natural or personal laws should be adhered to first. This tendency could suggest that psychopaths do not have strong moral laws laid out for themselves and are more inclined to only follow those of the systems in which they find themselves.

While there is no notable preference among psychopaths between the infliction of personal and interpersonal harm, these people are usually much less averse to inflicting interpersonal harm than are non-psychopaths. Those psychopaths with the lowest levels of anxiety are usually much more likely to inflict personal harm.

There are moderate genetic links or causes of psychopathy, but these are not quite as substantial as the environmental ones. The most common environmental causes of psychopathy all stem from early experiences in childhood and adolescence, including but not limited to coming from a disrupted family with a young or depressed mother, low involvement of the father, having convicted parents, physical neglect, low family income or social status, poor housing and or supervision, large family size, harsh discipline, and delinquent sibling(s).

Head injuries are also strongly linked with violence and psychopathy. It is the injuries to the prefrontal and orbitofrontal cortices that do the most harm to suffers, with impairments in social and moral reasoning being the most disconcerting effects of these injuries. Damage to the ventromedial cortex is also concerning, usually causing a reduction in autonomic responses, inability to make evasive maneuvers, impaired economic decision making, and diminished expressions of guilt, shame, and empathy.

Psychopathy is likely the most famous of the dark traits due to the destructiveness of its sufferers. Many of the world's most notorious criminals have been or are psychopathic, but this does not entail that all psychopaths are criminals. Some of them, in fact, go on to lead normal, productive lives in which they contribute greatly to society as a whole.

Now we come to sadism. Sadomasochism (or SM, as we will call it here) is the receiving of giving of pleasure stemming from the infliction of pain and or humiliation. Often sadists receive sexual gratification from the infliction of this pain, whether they are the ones giving it or the ones receiving it. These practices are, surprisingly, usually consensual, and so differ from non-consensual sex crimes.

The origin of the term sadism is found in Marquis De Sade (1740-1814), who both practiced sadistic sex rituals and wrote about them. The term masochism comes from Leopold Von Sacher-Masoch, who wrote novels about his own masochistic sex practices.

Some psychologists consider pain and violence to be at the center of the sadomasochistic practice, while others look more towards dominance and submission. In reality, most sadomasochists are interested in both. Sigmund Freud considered the first "form" of sadomasochism to be centered around the notion of cuckoldry (or the choosing of rivals as mates), and the second form to not concern itself with relationships at all and to be interested instead on the pageantry of the sexual practices.

Each sadomasochist finds the practices associated with the disorder appealing to his or her own reasons. Often, the SMs who prefer to take on more submissive roles within their practices do so out of a need to escape from the guilt, responsibility, and stress of life. Being in the presence of strong and domineering figures instills a sense of safety and security for others. Sadists, on the other hand, may enjoy taking on more domineering roles out of a desire to feel more empowered. Whether sadistic or masochistic, SMs are simply trying to fulfill emotional needs that they have, which often stem from childhood experiences and relationships. While these needs are met in ways some would find unusual or inappropriate, as long as these practices are consensual we will usually be wise to avoid judgment.

Finally, sociopathy (or antisocial personality disorder) is a personality disorder marked by a lack of remorse or guilt regarding wrongdoing inflicted onto others. This disorder is so similar to psychopathy that many psychologists in the past have considered it a sub disorder within a larger class of psychopathic disorders, but most today hold that sociopathy is a separate disorder all together. The same manipulation tactics, impulsivity, lack of guilt, and excess of aggression found in psychopaths and Machiavellians are shared by sociopaths.

While some sociopaths are high functioning and contribute great things to society, most have difficulties remaining responsible throughout life due to their impulsivity and often lead shorter lifespans than average as a result of reckless practices such as substance abuse and criminal activity.

While there is a noted genetic component to the development of antisocial personality disorder, there remains also certain environmental factors that can put young people at a greater risk of developing this disorder. These include but are not limited to never being taught to respect the rights of others, poor discipline, the presence of negative role models, and alcoholism as well as other forms of substance abuse, both in parents and in their children.

Conduct disorder and ADHD before the age of 10 is yet another indicator of later development of antisocial personality disorder. Some studies have even indicated that 25% of girls and 40% of boys who develop conduct disorder throughout development go on to develop antisocial personality disorder later on in adulthood.

The most common symptoms of sociopathy are as follows: the repeated committing of unlawful acts, lying or manipulating in order to achieve results, impulsivity, repeated fighting or assaults, disregard for the safety of the self and of others, a lack of empathy and remorse, and personal and financial irresponsibility. In order to be formally diagnosed with sociopathy, a person must exhibit at least three of the symptoms listed above. Other criteria that need to be met in order to diagnose one with antisocial personality disorder are that the person is at least 18 years old and that he or she has been diagnosed as having conduct disorder onset before or at the age of 15. Typically, there is some time of antisocial episode and a subsequent intervention taken place before a person is officially diagnosed with this disorder as most do not suspect of or admit to themselves having sociopathy. These episodes are not, however, necessary for a formal diagnosis of this troublesome disorder.

These symptoms usually peak when the sufferer is in his or her early twenties. Once he or she has reached the 40s, however, some find that these symptoms curtail and eliminate themselves.

Talk therapy is the most common and effective form of therapy for this disorder and is usually the same for all of the other dark personality traits. This form of therapy is helpful for these people because, in part, it offers a way for the individual to develop his or her interpersonal skills. The first goal within these therapies is, however, always the reduction of impulsive behaviors which may lead to criminal harm done.

There are surprisingly very little medications that help mitigate the symptoms of antisocial personality disorder. In addition, to talk therapy, clinicians also give schema therapies to many patents, which aim to edit and better organize maladaptive patterns of thought often stemming from childhood. The writer here would argue that this form of therapy should be more widely used among all those who suffer from dark personality traits, regardless of what those traits might be, though this is merely opinion.

Chapter three: Studies of dark psychology

There are no better assertions of dark psychological happenings than the actual studies conducted on the topic. We should now go over some of the most famous examples of such studies, pouring over both their reasons for having taken place and their significance after the fact.

The Asch experiments of the 1950s were conducted to ascertain to what degree an individual's opinions can be influenced by those of the majority of the group the individual finds him or herself in. Solomon Asch, the leader of these experiments, started these out by having young male college students participate in perceptual tasks. He divided the participants into groups, with all but one of the members in each group being "confederates" or actors. The goal of these experiments was to analyze how the one "genuine" participant would react to the thoughts and actions of all of the actors.

With all other participants having pre-scripted responses to all questions asked, the responses of the one genuine participant became the only true independent variables in the study. With varying degrees of peer pressure applied to the one real participant, the effects of this pressure were then seen and studied in their various degrees of severity.

Each participant was simply asked a series of questions, such as which line was the shortest or longer within a series. Initially, all of the "confederates" gave correct answers to all of the questions asked in order to avoid making the one genuine participant suspicious. It was only later on that some incorrect answers started to be added.

There was a control group among the normal groups when these experiments were taking place, in which no peer pressure was applied to participants. Within this control group, only around one out of every 35 answers were incorrect, a statistic likely attributable to mere experimental error. Within the normal groups, on the others hand, one third of the genuine participants gave an incorrect answer when others within the group had also done so. This implies that people are in fact much more likely to make incorrect judgments when the majority of those around them are doing the same.

At least ¾ of all participants gave at least one incorrect answer to the questions given to them. Within this experiment, people hid their own opinions, whether they were genuinely suspicious of their own intuitions, or were simply wanting to comply more with their company.

While we all tend to pride ourselves on being independently minded and fully autonomous individuals, studies like this one indicate that at times we behave like anything but. This issue of conformity vs. individuality is an age old struggle which some of the greatest minds in history have poured over tirelessly. Typically, moderation should be kept about when determining the relationship between our own opinions and those of the group(s) we find ourselves in. To trust our own intuitions entirely and without question would be arrogant, and could potentially plunge us into ignorance of the reality of our own making, one which could have easily been avoided by receptiveness to the opinions of others. We should also keep in mind that other people are just as susceptible to error as we are, and that might do not always make right. In following the pack blindly we are subjecting ourselves to whatever this pack may have in mind for us. Just because more people believe in something does not make that something more or less true. Bandwagons are great in that they make us feel like we are a part of something, but potentially destructive when we put too much faith in them.

It is not an example of personal darkness to deviate from the well-trodden paths of our company. While larger groups may provide order for their constituents, this order can easily become tyranny if not checked. When no one is around to verify the validity of any of the views of the group, the whole system tends to collapse in on itself, leaving the most dogmatic at the very bottom of the rubble. History gives us countless examples of people doing horrible things out of subservience to their tribe(s). The Asch experiments are merely a microcosmic reflection of this destructive tendency.

The bible tells one story of the good Samaritan, who stops to help a man in need while other, self-righteous people simply pass on by. John Darley and C. Daniel Batson, inspired by this famous story, wanted to see if there was any correlation between religiosity and helpfulness, and so conducted the good Samaritan experiment.

Three main hypotheses were on the researchers minds when heading into this experiment: that people thinking helpful religious thoughts would ultimately be no more inclined to help others than anyone else, that people who were in a rush would be less likely to help others, and that those who are religious simply for gain will be much less likely to help others than will people who are religious out of a want to find meaning in life. People of a Samaritan fashion will be more likely to help than people of a Levite fashion.

After recruiting seminary students for this experiment, the research conducted a questionnaire on religion on the participants in order to later ascertain the accuracy of the third hypothesis. They then started the experiment in one building, only to ask the participants to walk over to another building to finish the experiment. On the way there the participants found a man slumped over in an alleyway and had no knowledge of what was wrong with him or why he was there.

Before having the participants depart, they told different groups different pieces of information regarding urgency and what they would have to do in the other buildings. One of the tasks was related to seminary jobs and the other was related to the telling of the story of the good Samaritan. One of these groups was told that it was late and needed to head over to the other building right away, while the other group was told that it had a few minutes.

The man in the alleyway was cued to moan and cough twice while the participants passed by. The researchers set up a scale of helping beforehand which was organized as follows: 0= failure to notice the victim and his need, 1= noticing the need but offering no aid, 2= made no stop but did decide to help indirectly (telling their aide upon arrival), 3= stopping and asking the victim if he needed help, 4= stopping and helping the victim, leaving him aside afterwards, 5= refusing to leave the victim after stopping and offering help, or insistence on taking him somewhere else.

After the subjects arrived at the second location they had them answer a second questionnaire, this one regarding helpfulness. The sense of urgency had an effect on the helping of the man in the alleyway. All in all, around 40% of the participants chose to help the victim. Those who were not very rushed helped 63% of the time, those who were somewhat rushed helped 40% of the time, and those who were very rushed helped only 10% of the time. The Sammarinese here helped 53% of the time, while the Levites only helped 29% of the time, thereby confirming the third hypothesis. This study could ultimately find no correlation between religiosity and helpful behavior. Those who were more interested in helpfulness as a good in itself tended to be much more helpful than those who saw religion as a means of getting things that they wanted.

Even when on the way to give a speech about the good Samaritan, a person in a hurry is much less likely to help others around him or her. This just goes to show that thinking about ethics does not necessarily cause us to act more ethically. The relationship between urgency and helpfulness should also be taken note of, as this could indicate that as our lives are becoming more and more fast paced with each passing year we are bound to become less and less ethical, though this is just one take that could be had on this phenomena. There is one other possible explanation to the lack of help: the conflict between the needs of the experimenter vs. those of the victim could have affected the participants' decision making more so than any callousness on their part.

This experiment remains controversial in that it takes on religion, but only the unreasonable would deny that religion is better used by those who simply seek meaning in life than by those who are driven merely by avarice. There is simply no room for morality were people are desirous of more things. When we are overwhelmed by the multifarious wants that we have, we always open up pandora's box in order to meet them, letting all of the evilest things that we can imagine roam the earth simply out of greed. Charity really is a good in of itself. From a utilitarian standpoint, it is almost always better to be more charitable because the happiness derived from doing so is not only felt in our beneficiaries but in ourselves as well.

This study also shows us that in order to promote the good and avoid the bad we are going to have to take time out of our days to do so. Haste in our actions makes us much less likely to help others. When we are constantly busy with our own activities we sometimes fail to recognize the needs of others, but stopping to do so every once in a while will benefit us greatly in the long run.

The bystander apathy experiment of 1968 conducted by John Darley and Bibb Latane sought to explore one of the most interesting, and perhaps disappointing, phenomena in the field of social psychology. Within this type of experiment, an emergency is staged with one participant among several other confederates. These researchers would then study how long it took the participant to act if he or she chose to do so at all. Surprisingly, this study showed us all that we are much less likely to help others when in the company of a crowd. Around 70% of participants helped when no others were involved, while only 40% chose to do so in the company of groups.

This reluctance to help others when in crowds may stem from mere self-consciousness, or it could also be due to a perception that being the one who helps first is to take on something of a leadership role, a role which most people are averse to taking up for themselves. For whatever reason it may occur, this tendency to neglect those in need is problematic for obvious reasons. No matter what the trouble happens to be, we are more likely to avoid it when we find ourselves in larger groups, as this experiment would seem to suggest.

The Stanford prison experiment, perhaps the most well-known of any mentioned here, was conducted in 1971 by Philip Zimbardo with an aim to study what psychological effects are entailed in becoming either a prisoner or a prison guard. Here 24 male subjects were taken and randomly selected to be either guards or prisoners within a mock prison in the basement of the Stanford psychology building.

Zimbardo was reportedly impressed at how quickly the subjects adapted to their roles, as the guards quickly took on more and more authoritarian roles and eventually even resorted to the psychological torture of the prisoners. Not only did the prisoners take the psychological abuse passively, they even went so far as to harass other prisoners at the requests of the guards. It was not until after Zimbardo himself started to condone the abuse that two prisoners quit the experiment early and it was all stopped after only six days.

Impressionability and obedience tend to rise greatly when people have access to an ideology that makes them feel legitimized and institutional and social support, as this study would suggest. This study also goes to show the effects of cognitive dissonance and the power of authority. When we are under the control of a system that we perceive as having a strong, centralized basis of power, we tend to become very willing to follow the wants of that system, whatever they might be. We also become highly impressed upon by that system. When conflicts of interests between ourselves and the will of the system arise, cognitive dissonance follows, which is resolved by more obedience in most people. This study also demonstrates our tendency to let authority figures get away with doing whatever they have in mind.

This study is considered situational rather than dispositional behaviors, meaning that the behaviors noted here we more a result of the situation at hand than one of the personalities of the participants. Whether the guards had a disposition towards committing abuse, or whether the prisoners were disposed towards passivity is not a matter of concern here. The only thing studied here is the situational behavior of those involved.

This study tells us so much about prison life. To reflect on what would have happened had the guards never been stopped does raise some other questions though. It is not clear what would have ever checked the power of Zimbardo in this study. He had the power to essentially do anything to the subjects, so this study can also be analyzed as an inquiry into the issue of unchecked power.

The Milgram experiments of 1961, conducted by Stanley Milgram, is one of the most insightful studies of authority in the field of social psychology. Here the objective was to record the willingness of participants to perform tasks that went against their own personal consciousness when these tasks had been assigned by an authority figure.

Milgram conducted these experiments with the trials of Nazi war criminals in mind, asking himself one central question: did all of these war criminals have a shared sense of morality? These studies, on the whole, confirmed that people often perform actions that go against their strongest moral beliefs when compelled to by authority figures. While these studies proved to be scientifically valid and useful, many considered and still consider them to have been unethical, entailing both physical and psychological abuse that scared the participants for life.

Milgram recruited 40 men to take part in these experiments. These was a shock generator used, the shocks of which started at 30 volts and increased by 15 volt increments until finally reaching 450, many of them owning such labels as "slight shock", "moderate shock", and "danger: severe shock". The final two switched on this generator were simply labeled "xxx".

These participants of this experiment took on the role of the "teacher", who would administer shocks when the confederates would give incorrect answers given to them. Although these shocks were not really administered, the teachers believed them to be and the confederates would act as though they had been shocked when they were administered.

As the voltage would continually increase as the experiment went on, the student would ask to be released and some would even complain of heart conditions. Once the 300 volt threshold had been crossed over, the student would start to bang on the walls of the room and would thereafter refuse to answer any further questions. This silence, as the teachers were instructed, was supposed to be taken as an incorrect answer, so more shocks were administered when the questions were not answered.

Most of the students asked the teachers whether or not they should continue, to which they were given the standard replies: "please continue", "the experiment requires that you continue", "it is absolutely essential that you continue", and "you have no other choice, you must continue".

The level of shock that each participant was willing to deliver was the indicator of their obedience. It was initially predicted that only around 3 out of every 100 participants would agree to administer the maximum shocks. In reality, an astonishing 65% of them would actually go on to administer these shocks, and each participant involved would administer the 300 volt shocks. This shows that people are even more compliant than most expect them to be and that we can easily be compelled to actions that we find objectionable when under the influence of authority figures.

The Milgram experiment shows us that we are, in many cases, willing to go so far as to kill others if instructed to do so by an authority figure who we deem to have moral and or legal authority. This obedience is learned early on in life within us and is adapted and reinforced in many different ways throughout the courses of our lives. We all know that we naturally tend to go with wishes of those who have more power than us, but the Milgram experiments teach us just to what extend this tendency carries through within our actions.

According to Milgram, we fall into one of two states behaviorally within social situations: the autonomous state (in which people direct their own actions) and the agentic state (in which people let others direct their actions). Milgram asserts that we need the following criteria to be met for us to enter into the agentic state of behavior: the person giving orders is perceived as being qualified, and that the order taker trusts the ordered to take responsibility for anything that goes wrong.

Agency theory suggests that it is only when we feel responsible for our own actions that we truly start to act with autonomy. While putting responsibility into the hands of others may be relieving, we have to be responsible for what we are doing if we are to remain autonomous actors.

The studies here mentioned, among many others, show the darker underbelly of the human psyche. While it may be hard to accept that we are flawed in the ways that these studies prove us to be, doing so will always lead us to better and more honest lives, fully aware of our both our unassailable successes and catastrophic failures.

Chapter four: Mind reading

Mind reading is mainly a game of three factors: sensory information, in-person body cues, and social cues. Without attention paid to these three aspects of communication any attempt at delving into the thoughts and feelings of others becomes fruitless. Today we typically communicate more so through text messages, IMs, emails, and phone calls than through real interpersonal conversations. This entails that we tend to miss out on learning the finer points of real communications, and are subsequently far less able to tell what others are thinking. Screen time seems to be the most destructive thing for us in the way of telling what others are thinking.

For better or worse, we can usually tell what others are thinking with or without the aid of what they are actually saying. The words are often just the tip of the iceberg when it comes to what is actually going on within other people's minds. When most hear the term "mind reading" they tend to think of psychics, witches, and other people of this sort, but great steps can be taken by anyone to better understand the thoughts of others. With just a little guidance and a lot of practice, anyone can become just as proficient in the art of telling what others are thinking as the more mystical figures among us.

So much of interpersonal human connection is dependent upon our ability to guess at and respond to the thoughts and actions of others appropriately that we often have difficulty reconciling what is actually being said by others with what impressions we are getting from them. In order to understand the thoughts of others, we must first delve into our own. It is all too easy for an attempt at understanding what another person is thinking to quickly turn into a judgment. We jump to conclusions about the people we meet and often run into errors as a result.

One of the greatest obstacles we face we trying to mind read is that of dishonesty or a lack of expression in the words or the nonverbal cues of those who we are talking to. When we come across people with good poker faces and or dishonest people, our tendency gauge language and nonverbal cues are of little use to us. There are, however, many ways in which we can dig beneath the superficial aspects of the communication and get a glimpse at what it really going on within our partner's minds.

In order to read minds, we must first trust our own intuition. This involves developing a more trustworthy intuition though, which is a task that is always becoming and never being. Here we should avoid some of the magical thinking that often goes into the habit of mind reading and only use our reason. A willingness to look into the places that we least want to and to challenge our own beliefs is also crucial here because if we go into trying to read the minds of others already anchored to our own beliefs our findings will always be less fruitful. For example, if I am convinced of the pretentiousness of a person right at meeting them and never think to challenge this conviction, I will never be granted greater insight into their character because I have already categorized them. We do not need to have esoteric powers in order to mind read, we only need to be open and reasonable when communicating with others.

Mindfulness is one of the greatest skills that we can home in on in order to read minds more effectively. This practice allows us to clear our minds of any needless distractions and worries, enabling us to pay greater attention to those who we are speaking with. When we have our heads fully grated on our own inner worries and problems we can never delve into what is going on with others fully. Any ability that we may have had in the way of understanding other people's thoughts falls by the wayside as we try to pick up our own pieces with cluttered and anxiety riddled psyches. Here it becomes clear that if we want to determine what is going on within other people's inner lives we are first going to have to look at our own. Doing so will give us the clarity and the energy necessary for reading the minds of others.

The first step towards better reading the minds of others is always to maintain an open spirit for doing so. Without this openness, we will never reap the full rewards of what other people are communicating to us. This openness does necessarily have to come with a certain degree of intolerance though, intolerance directed at anything that does not immediately serve whatever purposes we have in the present moment. When we try to take in all things, including those things that have nothing to do with us, we always get overwhelmed and feel as though we are making no progress toward our goals, because we probably are not. When we instead remain open only to the things that are affecting us directly we usually find that we have much more energy to understand others and to work with what we have accordingly.

Again, mindfulness training of some kind is the best practice we have to foster this sense of openness. Stress and distraction cause us to not only extract less information out of others but to also misinterpret what little that we do get. Any interpretations of other people's thoughts that we make when under stress are inherently ill conceived and hindered by our own issues. As Kant believed, it is only the judgments of the unprejudiced that should be taken into account, so mindfulness is a necessary practice for all those who want to better read minds.

Next, we have to determine who it is whose mind we want or need to read. If we come out of the gates swinging, so to speak, trying to tell what is going on within everyone's inner lives, then we are invariably bound to experience a great deal of pushback and make more than a few enemies in the process. We should go about determining our people strategically if the situation calls for it. If we are in need of a best man for a wedding, for example, it will not serve our purpose to read the minds of the women who we meet at the supermarket. This may sound like a Machiavellian line of reasoning, but we can only read so many people's minds, so we should be selective about who we try to do so to and use our powers for good.

When we have our person/people in mind, the first indicators of their characters and thinking patterns we are granted are found in their external appearances. Details like their face(s), body language, posture, and clothing should be paid attention to. Typically, a person's outward appearance is an accurate reflection of their inward life, though there are many exceptions to this rule. Many modern philosophers consider us all to be cultural constructs, always being influenced and even shaped into what we are by the culture that surrounds us. This is why we can often tell much more about a person by what they look like on the outside than many pop culture platitudes would tend to suggest that we can. What more, we are always making political statements in what we wear, consume, and associate with, so these items can act as great indicators of what we are truly like as well.

While some of the people whose minds we try to read are premeditated figures (meaning we have made up our minds beforehand to analyze them), other people just seem to jump out at us, begging for our attention by how they look, act, and seem to think. This is one of the main reasons why mind reading is always being and never becoming because the "truths" that we hold about people are constantly being shaped by the whole of people we know, within both old relationships and new. We ultimately cannot divorce our understanding of one person or group from any of the others we know. All of them our inextricably linked one to the other by our understanding as a whole.

When we see other people, there are two main categories in which our minds our perceiving our external reality: what is the person and what is not the person. While the setting that the person is within may contain insights into who the person truly is, we still need to differentiate between the person and whatever setting this might be. It is impossible to do this fully because sense perception is ultimately confused and disorganized, but once sense perception is made clearer by abstracting from its individuality and singularity (in this case separating the individual from the setting) it becomes higher order cognition. The point here is to not let other things in the background influence our own perceptions of the people we are communicating with.

With this laser-like focus given to the person we are communicating with, we can flush out any of the distracting background information that we are taking in, better enabling us to truly understand what is going on inside the person's head. When our energies become diluted by needless background worries we lose our ability to see clearly what others are thinking.

We should always make these decisions as to who to read carefully because we are constantly being shaped by those around us. The people who we spend the most time with and who we pay attention to most closely are always going to shape our characters much more than any others. Those who we read most closely should not only be the ones who offer us the most, but they should also be the ones who encourage us to be our best selves the most. In this way, we can become much better people merely by following those who we most admire/ get along with.

Once we are engaged with another communicator, we need to maintain our focus on the person. This includes making eye contact: a task that most are not willing to carry through with. Around 15 seconds is the ideal amount of time to maintain eye contact with a person upon meeting them. Any more time tends to make others uncomfortable, while any less does not foster a great connection with the other.

Once this eye contact has been made we should formulate a mental image of who we have made contact with. We should take note of and remember the face of the person we have met, as well as the energy they have given off. We should let the thoughts and emotions on the person's face make an impression on us. This should be done with the same sense of openness as all the stages of this practice are, as we have to accept all of the impressions that we get from the other, whether good or bad and also cannot skim over any of these bad impressions that we get without any self-criticism.

Once we have made initial contact with the person in this more analytical manner we can start to truly read the thoughts of the other. Doing this with any justice done to the person at hand involves keeping a certain amount of receptiveness and cooperation. Conversing with another is supposed to be a two way street, on which there is a negotiated and equal dialogue among parties. Where most people run into trouble is in their proclivity toward valuing their own points above those of any others. This is where a large portion of interpersonal conflict arises, where people only want to focus on their own ideas and never think to listen to those of others.

We should typically trust and follow our own intuition while conversing with others. This requires honesty and openness, and also a fair amount of security, as we never know how much other people are trying to read us. Conversations, as we all know, tend to work best when all parties are on the same page, but without transparency, there is never any determining whether or not we are in agreement with those who we are speaking with. We are rational actors capable of defending ourselves wherever we need to do so, so we should never feel threatened moving into new conversations and relationships, even if the other parties may be working toward malevolent ends.

Allowing any thoughts to come our way from others is the only way to ensure that we are getting maximum information out of what is being said. Those who look into the bad or disagreeable thoughts here will be rewarded in the long run for doing so. To ignore the scary or dark thoughts of others is just as maladaptive as ignoring the good ones. We should avoid holding anything against the other person upon meeting them, but whatever bad things that present themselves should be looked into. It should also be noted that often times when we feel scared or uncomfortable by something it is a good indication that we are about to learn something that we do not already know. The disagreeable things that we come across usually teach us much more than do the nice things, so we should look into and feel deeply the worse thoughts of others.

Our own emotional intelligence needs to be fostered if we are going to make any attempts at reading the thoughts of others. When we cannot pinpoint our own thoughts and aspirations, as we often cannot, we are not able to pinpoint those of others. Looking at our reasoning behind the thoughts we have will enable us to solve our own problems and to then ascertain what we would like out of other people. We are always in a negotiated dialogue with others around us, always sending out signals as to how we expect to be dealt with, as well as receiving signals as to how others expect us to deal with them. When we do not know what we are thinking and what we want the former half of this dialogue is never met, and we are consequently left only with information as to what others want from us, never having asserted our own appetites and aversions.

All too many listeners listen only to respond rather than to understand. This draws back to our tendency to only take our own ideas into account while conversing with others. People are able to tell a notable difference between these two types of listeners, and putting our own responses above understanding is always a surefire way to put people off of us, often times for good. Everyone has interjections to make at all points within a conversation. Those who are less secure and more dependent upon external validation are much more likely to pay attention to their own interjections than to what is actually being said. Those who listen to others with genuine reception and curiosity, only interested in getting a clear picture of the content of what is being said, are a rare breed in a solipsistic world polluted by needless opinions and assertions, and one that is increasingly valued and sought after by all.

Listening more than we speak is another step that we can take in the same vein as the last one. While those who limit their interjections in social situations may not immediately gain the same reverence as others, these people do usually end up absorbing more information than others. Constantly speaking reduces the value of our own words. The paradox of speech is found where this desire to gain visibility through our speech by over speaking causes us to become invisible. When entering a conversation we should keep in mind that, unless we are teaching or instructing, our main job is usually to listen. While this may not seem as glamorous as speaking constantly, it does usually offer much more rewards, and while we may not gain admiration for our erudition in the short term, in the long term silence will make us wise, and we will usually appear so to others.

Most people are choosing to become less empathetic as time goes on. It is noted that this is a choice because it takes very little effort, in reality, to identify with others. Empathy is reciprocal, meaning that when we empathize with others they become much more likely to do the same with us. So many interpersonal problems are constructed merely out of conflicting parties working towards their own interests without stepping back for a second and considering what it is that the others are thinking. Mind reading is largely a game of empathy, one that rewards being able to identify with other people's qualms and work with them towards common goals. In order to empathize well, however, we need to put our own thoughts first, otherwise, we are bound to simply serve others in our relationships.

If we are going to make further progress on reading the thoughts of others we are going to have to analyze them holistically. This is where some problems will always arise because no two people are exactly the same. People are complicated, and just when we think we have figured out another fully, yet another layer of the onion that is their personality is peeled away, asking us to strip away axiomatic preconceptions and other facets of our integrated knowledge structure in order to adapt to the changes that we are met with.

One of the biggest differences that can occur between two or more people is a generational difference or one of age. All generations have (sometimes dramatically) different interpersonal styles. A generation Xer, for example, is usually going to prefer face to face contact, while a millennial will often prefer contact through social media, text, etc.

Taking a person's generation into account will help us to better conduct affairs with them. This extends to both how we should speak to them and what we should speak about. People are inclined toward nostalgia, so we will typically be better off speaking about the 1950s with a baby boomer than with a homelander. Most communication today is done via technology, so we should expect to have conversations with younger people through our devices more so than those with older people. Here we should cater to the wants of others while also ensuring that we have room for our own interests and peculiarities.

Hot buttons are another thing to keep note of, as there are very few things that will close a person up as a conversationalist quite like squishing their opinions regarding these issues that they hold convictions about so dearly. After we do so we run the risk of remaining in a conversation with a person whose opinion(s) we have squashed, which is never an ideal situation to find ourselves within. We should look for what bothers and pains others out of a desire to either avoid these topics or to render whatever aid we can muster, not to pour salt into wounds and to add insult to injury. Here again, empathy comes into play, the ability to see and understand why people feel the way they do about these topics.

The issues that we find most important are incredibly reflective of our character. When someone takes a firm stance on something we should take their opinion seriously because odds are that they have thought about the subject more than we have ourselves. Most people are surprisingly insightful, especially when it comes to issues that they feel beg their attention. It is much too easy to get caught up in the heat of the moment and to insult others for their views, but this mode of conduct does not help interpersonal connections.

Next, we should take note of the individual personalities that we are dealing with. This can be the hardest step because a personality is an incredibly complex and multifaceted construction that cannot be merely glanced over once. While first impressions usually give us pretty reliable indications of what a person is really like, we always have to delve much deeper into a person than what meets the eye if we want to determine how to conduct ourselves around them.

We have to make some concerted effort to tailor our conversational style to the personality style that we are in contact with. This entails ascertaining what a person is like fundamentally and adjusting our communication directed at them accordingly. Here the MBTI personality types can be used to our advantage. This system categorizes personalities in terms of four categories: favorite world (introversion or extraversion), information (sensing or intuition), decisions (thinking or feeling), and structure (judging or perceiving).

Extraverts tend to focus most of their energies into their outer worlds, whereas introverts prefer to introspect. People who sense usually focus only on the pure information they are given, while those who intuit usually add their own interpretations and meaning. Thinkers tend to consider consistency and logic while making decisions, while feelers look more at people involved and special circumstances. When observing the outside world, judges tend to want to get things decided whereas perceivers prefer to stay open to new information. All of these personality dimensions should be kept in mind when conversing with others because these dimensions can create large chasms between people that will have to be crossed.

Looking into the verbiage that a person uses, as well as his or her tone of voice, is a great way to gain insights into the personality of who you are speaking with. By using these tools we can dig deeper and deeper down into the understory of the other person as well as the relationship that we have with them. Without using these tools we are left blind in our search for how to better deal with the person.

Nonverbal communication should also continually be addressed. This form of communication is always taken note of when we first meet a new person, but all too many of us let this notice fall by the wayside as relationships develop. Paying continued attention to this form of communication will always give great rewards to those who choose to do so. The main areas of concern to be taken into account while observing nonverbal communication are the use of eye contact, the use of time, of touch, of voice, the use of physical appearance/environment, distance, and body language.

Encoding and decoding are the two processes used in transmitting and deciphering nonverbal language respectively. These processes can take place either consciously or unconsciously. The signals are given off while encoding are usually ones that we perceive to be universal, while those registered during decoding depend on the disposition of the encoder. Nonverbal communication is also heavily influenced by culture. We learn certain nonverbal cues, by both encoding and decoding, from a young age and continue on using most of these cues throughout our lives. Every society has its own set of nonverbal cues, but there are certain universal regulators of this type of communication applicable to all people.

An astonishing two thirds of all communication is done through nonverbal means. This means that this supposedly subordinate form of communication is, in reality, more important that verbal communication. Most of the time nonverbal cues will match the content of speech rather well, though there is often divergence in the signals produced by these two forms of communication. This divergence can be resultant of deceit, poor communicative ability, or just a lack of overall communication by the encoder. It is usually the nonverbal cues that are most accurate to follow in these cases, as 83% of what we perceive is given to us by sight, 11% by hearing, 3% by smell, 2% by touch, and 1% by taste.

It only takes one tenth of a second for someone to judge another upon meeting them and to make their first impression. First impressions are usually produced nonverbally and tend to last a long time in their effectiveness. There are both positive and negative first impressions, both of which are usually made through the presentation of the other person in terms of appearance and what he or she is saying, and through the personal prejudices of the individual being impressed upon. Though these impressions are often misleading, especially when given to the prejudiced, they are more often than not pretty accurate representations of the people giving off the impressions.

When most think of nonverbal communication, the first aspect of it that comes to mind is posture. Body posture can often tell more about what is going on inside of a person's mind than the words they speak will. These postures usually include things such as crouching, arm crossing, shoulders forward, jaw trust, legs spread, and towering. Before analyzing the body language of others we should first go over a few tips as to how to better our own body language.

Facial expressions are one of the most important factors in making first impressions. By starting a relationship off with a smile, you are associating yourself with positivity. 48 percent of Americans claim that a person's smile becomes their most memorable trait after meeting them. Sometimes excessive smiling can seem unauthentic or even arrogant but smiling authentically always tends to charm.

Not only does smiling make good first impressions more accessible, but it also is shown to decrease levels of stress hormones such as cortisol and adrenaline. Smiling is not only friendly, but it is also one of the main keys to longevity.

A proper handshake remains one of the tenants of politeness the world over. Giving a good one, however, depends on maintaining that important balance between being too firm and too soft. If a healthy medium is established than you will make much better first impressions.

Verbal introductions are the most important part of the first seven seconds spent with someone. There are plenty of common introductions in our vernacular, these include 'hello', 'nice to meet you', etc. Whichever one you use; a verbal introduction can help very much to break the silence and tension involved in meeting someone new.

A common issue that lots of people are confronted with in meeting new people is that they lack the confidence to speak clearly. Speaking timidly is not only an easy way to be overlooked but it also often leads to being taken less seriously. It has been shown that those who speak in a deeper and calmer voice are usually taken more seriously, so find a balance between whispering and screaming and you will tend to create better relationships.

Eye contact shows others that you are not only interested in what they are saying, but that you are also confident in yourself. Eye contact is also a great indicator of respect among people. It is, however, to be used in moderation though. Too much eye contact can intimidate a person or make them feel uncomfortable, while looking away may be construed as a distraction.

Body language is, more often than not, mirrored when two people are talking to one another. Your smile, for example, is mirrored by those around you by means of a specialized neuron responsible for mirroring facial expressions. This establishes between the two of you mutual understanding, connection, and trust. Other usages of positive body language are helpful as well, especially when carried out within the first seven seconds of meeting a new person.

Your attire can be a huge indicator of what you are like to a new person. If you dress in clothes that make you feel comfortable and confident people are more likely to perceive you as being that way. The opposite, however, is also true. Not only will dressing well help you to make better first impressions, but it will also improve your mood and your confidence.

In the words of Dale Carnegie, "We should be aware of the magic contained in a name and realize that this single item is wholly and completely owned by the person with whom we are dealing and nobody else." People very much enjoy hearing their own names, even more so than they usually realize. Hearing one's own name can especially stick out to people in the modern era, which is so overwhelming in its excess of names and information. Once you remember someone's name, it is always a good idea to keep calling that person by their name as this you make you seem more agreeable.

This is an aspect of life that people tend to neglect. Ask yourself what your own goals are in meeting any given new person. A clear vision of what these goals might be will give you more of an idea of how to set your tone and behave around this person. This will also make it much easier to communicate with others because you will have a better idea of what you are communicating.

No one wants to talk to a person who is not interested in what they have to say or who does not think before he or she speaks. This is why it is important to err on the side of viewing others as potential teachers and also to be precise in what you have to say. It will make others more inclined to want to talk to you if you show empathy for them and try to give them only the best of what you have to say. Showing thoughtfulness in your words or actions is one of the best ways of making a lasting impression on others.

Bad moods can make unexpectedly strong impressions on people. If you are meeting a new person but are in a bad mood for whatever reason, try your hardest to leave your negativity behind you. It is always amazing how easily negative attitudes can rub off on others around you.

Chapter five: Cognitive psychology

The main focus of the cognitive approach to psychology is the study of mental processes, including but not limited to thinking, creativity, problem solving, perception, memory, language use, and attention. The focus on the mental processes of humans can be seen all the way back in ancient Greece with Plato, the first philosopher on record to assert that the brain is the seat of human mental processes. Rene Descartes would later add to our understanding of the mind with his conviction that all humans are born with innate ideas, as well as with his notion of a mind-body dualism of human beings. After these two thinkers, one of the most popular debates in philosophy would become one of the notions of experiential thought (empiricism) vs. that of innate ideas (nativism). In the 19th century, George Berkeley and John Locke would argue on the side of the empiricists while Immanuel Kant would be the main proponent of the nativist view.

The next large step to be made in the field of cognitive psychology was Paul Broca's discovery of a certain area of the brain responsible for the production of language. This leap was promptly followed by a similar one in which Carl Wernicke discovered another area largely responsible for language comprehension. Both of these areas were then named after their founders and maladaptation and trauma to these areas causing disruptions to an individual's production of language or comprehension is called Broca's aphasia or Wernicke's aphasia to this day.

The 1920s to the 1950s saw a rise in the popularity of behaviorism. The first adherents of the school of thought considered things such as consciousness, attention, ideas, and thoughts to be unobservable and outside of the realm of psychological study. While the behaviorist view had its strong points, it also contained its demerits and Jean Piaget was the first notable figure of the time to go against the grain of the school and to study the intelligence, language, and thoughts of individual children and adults.

The WW2 area saw the founding of information theory, the study of the communication, storage, and quantification of information within the brain. This proved to be of more use in tracking the performance of soldiers fighting on the fronts than behaviorism, which had no explanation of how well troops would fair in combat. The development of AI would later have a profound influence on psychological thought, as many psychologists started at once to see parallels between computerized "brains" and those of humans in the areas of memory storage and retrieval. The cognitive revolution of the 1950s, initiated by Noam Chomsky, created the field of cognitive science by analyzing the production of thought processes through a multidisciplinary lens including maxims within the fields of anthropology, linguistics, and psychology.

The term "cognition" is a blanket term used to refer to all processes in which sensory input is used, recovered, stored, elaborated, transformed, and reduced. Even when these processes are bereft of sensory information they remain active, often manifesting images and sometimes hallucinations. With this broad definition, it becomes clear that cognition is involved in everything that a person does. There are, however, still different ways of analyzing thought processes that deviate from this cognitive approach, including the dynamic approach, which would analyze a subject's instincts, needs, or goals rather than his or her beliefs, remembrances, or visions when taking actions or experiences into account.

Cognitive psychology analyzes mental processes with the main objective of looking into behavior. The first mental process that cognitive psychologists take into account is that of attention, in which awareness is keenly focused on a mere subset of the perceptual information available to a person. Here irrelevant information is filtered out from the more important things going on, giving the individual greater power to analyze specific sensory input. The human brain can cognize tactile, taste, olfactory, visual, and audio information at once, but it is only when a select amount of this information is focused on that we can clarify this information.

There are two main attentional systems used within our mind: exogenous and endogenous control. Exogenous control focuses more on pop-out effects and orienting reflex, while endogenous control focuses more on conscious processing and divided attention.

Divided attention is one of the focal points of cognitive psychology. While divided attention does make information processing more difficult, we still do retain the ability to perform tasks when we have a lot on our plate, so to speak. The cocktail party effect attests to this notion, asserting that we are able to carry on conversations and pay attention to their contents in environments in which there are many more conversations taking place. The information being shadowed done, however, fall by the wayside, leaving our memory as soon as we cognize it.

The next process that cognitive psychologists look into is that of memory. There are two main types of memory: long term memory and short term, both containing their own subtypes therein. Short term memory will here be referred to as working memory, as this is the verbiage most commonly used within the field today.

Working memory, while typically used interchangeably with short term memory as a term, refers to our ability to take in information when distractions are present. This form of memory consists of a central executive burg of memory that is interconnected inextricably with a phonological loop of language, a visuospatial sketchpad of visual semantics, and an episodic buffer of short-term episodic memories. The main issue of memory is forgetting. Cognitive psychology offers us two competing solutions to this problem: decay theory which asserts that memories leave us after a while due merely to the passage of time, and interference theory which asserts that memories leave us due to their being interfered with by others pieces of information being brought in as time goes on.

Next, we have long-term memory, of which there are three main subclasses. Procedural memory is the memory used for the completion of tasks which takes place either unconsciously or requires a minimal amount of conscious effort. This type of memory contains stimulus response information that is used to perform certain tasks or routines. This type of memory makes the seemingly automated completion of tasks and routines possible. Driving a car and riding a bicycle are two great examples of actions performed with this type of memory used.

Next, we come to semantic memory. This is the type of memory wherein our more encyclopedic knowledge is found. Pieces of information that we pick up over the years through diverse sources are incorporated into our stores of this type of memory. For example, our knowledge of types of turtles in our area or what the leaning Tower of Pisa looks like would be stored in our semantic memory. The access granted to us of these pieces of information within this system of memory is dependent on a number of factors, including how recently the piece of information was gained, the level of its meaning, its frequency of access, and the number of associations that it may have with other pieces of information. We typically remember the most recent and salient of our memories, paying extra attention to the pieces of information that affect us directly and profoundly in the present moment.

Finally, episodic memory is used to store and recall autobiographical sketches that can be explicitly stated by the individual. This type of memory contains temporal memories only, such as when a person brushed his or her teeth last and when the individual purchased his or her first car. Retrieving memories from this type of memory takes more conscious effort than to do the same with memories of other types, as it is necessary to combine both temporal information and semantic memories to paint the pictures of what we are trying to find. This is, however, arguably the most important type of long term memory due to the fact that it contains bother the temporal information and the semantic memory previously mentioned.

Now we come to the process of perception. This process entails the interpretation, identification, and organization of sensory input (of propriotation, touch, sight, smell, hearing, and taste) and the reconciliation of the individual cognitive processes that go into those sensory channels. The earliest studies of this process were done by structuralists such as Edward Titchener, who attempted to reduce all of the human thought to its most basic constituent components by observing how individuals respond to sensory stimuli.

Metacognition is, broadly, the thoughts that an individual has about his or her own thoughts themselves. For example, metacognition would be used under the following circumstances: the effectiveness of a person in determining his or her own capabilities of performance of certain tasks, a person's introspective understanding or his or her own strengths and weaknesses in performing certain mental tasks, and a person's ability to employ cognitive strategies to solve problems.

Where the study of metacognition proves to be most useful is within the field of education. A student's ability to cognize objectively his or her own thinking patterns has repeated been linked to better study and learning habits. One of the main reasons for this correlational existence lies within the student's added ability to set and meet goals through self-regulation. Metacognitive tasks are a great way to ensure that students are accurately assessing the degree of their own knowledge and gaining skills in their goal setting abilities.

Some of the most common phenomena related to metacognition are Deja Vu (the feeling of repeating experience), cryptomnesia (the unconscious plagiarism of past thoughts combined with the belief of their novelty and uniqueness), the false fame effect (the making out of non-famous names to be in fact famous), the validity effect (wherein repeated exposure to statements seems to give them more validity), and imagination inflation (the imagining of an event that never in fact occurred with the confidence that it did occur increasing over time).

Dual process theory asserts that thoughts can come from two different processes. The first of these processes is implicit and unconscious and occurs automatically, while the second is explicit and conscious, occurring under controlled conditions.

Modern social psychology owes much of its knowledge to earlier studies done by cognitive psychologists. The sub-set of social psychology that is most inextricably linked with the field of cognitive psychology is that of social cognition, which studies the ways in which people store, process, and applies information regarding particular people and social situations. This sub-set helps us understand human interactions on a basis that would never have otherwise been possible.

Theory of mind, broadly, deals with the ability of an individual to attribute and understand the cognition of those around them. This theory is especially useful in the field of developmental psychology, where analyzing this ability in developing children and adolescents is essential for predicting and determining behavioral patterns being applied within social situations. Cognitive psychology intermingles with developmental psychology effortlessly because our ability to cognize asserts itself from the start of our lives. Theory of mind, on the other hand, only starts to occur around the ages of four to six, due to the fact that this is usually when a child starts to recognize that he or she has his or her own thoughts and therefore other people must have thoughts of their own. Theory of mind is essentially a form a metacognition in that it requires that we analyze our own thoughts as well as those of others.

Jean Piaget was the first developmental psychologist to prognosticate the theory of cognitive development. This theory analyzes the development of human intelligence as a person develops into an adult.

Educational psychology has also been profoundly influenced by the field of cognitive psychology. Metacognition is analyzed in educational psychology in terms of self-monitoring, which keeps track of how accurately students monitor their own performance when learning and developing new skills. This also entails the analysis of how well they apply the knowledge of their own shortcomings to better this performance.

Declarative and procedural knowledge is also analyzed in educational psychology. Declarative knowledge is more like the cumulative encyclopedic knowledge that we gain throughout the years, whereas procedural knowledge deals more with knowledge of how to perform certain tasks and or pieces of information relating to these tasks. One of the most daunting tasks that many educational psychologists face throughout their careers is getting children and adolescents to integrate declarative knowledge into their systems of procedural knowledge.

Knowledge organization is another ongoing issue in the field of educational psychology. The knowledge of how knowledge is organized and sorted in the brain gained by cognitive psychologists has greatly benefitted the field of educational psychology. This organization takes place in a series of hierarchies that prove to be of much use for educational psychologists to keep in mind in their work.

Cognitive psychology is, as the name would suggest, much more concerned with the concepts of applied psychology than cognitive science is. It is also differentiated from this field of science in that it attempts to analyze psychological phenomena. Cognitive psychologists are often in the study of how the human brain absorbs, processes, and bases decision making on the input granted to it. The information that they obtain within this study is usually kept and applied within the field of clinical psychology. This field of psychological study is unique in that it is so strongly linked with the fields of linguistics, philosophy, artificial intelligence, neuroscience, and anthropology.

We could argue that the role of cognitive science is subordinate to that of cognitive psychology. This would be justified because much (if not most) of the findings of cognitive scientists are only used within the field of cognitive psychology. Work done in this field can sometimes be of more use than any done in cognitive psychology due to the fact that cognitive scientists often perform experiments on other animals that would be considered unethical to perform on humans.

The earliest criticisms of cognitive psychology came from behaviorists, who generally disagreed with the empiricism of the field, finding it to be incompatible with the existence of mental states. The answer to this criticism was later most sharply expressed in the sub field of cognitive neuroscience, which found evidence of direct correlations between real, physiological brain activity and determinative mental states.

Another major research area within cognitive psychology is the process of categorization. This process entails the recognition, differentiation, and understanding of the substrate of objects and ourselves as subjects. This process is needed to draw differences and similarities between things in our observable reality. Where some of us start to see issues is, however, when this categorization of objects and subjects starts to make two facts within a continuum indistinguishable, causing paradoxes in contradictory statements wherever they present themselves.

Within our power of judgment sits or the ability of induction and acquisition, which allows us to lean concepts by discerning exemplars from non-exemplars. The abilities to distinguish similarities and differences between objects and to represent, classify and structure what we draw in from sensory experience is also found within our power of judgment. This power does, however, subordinate to the power of understanding, meaning that none of these abilities are possible without understanding.

Cognitive psychology also researches the area of knowledge representation and reasoning. This area of thought gives us the ability to represent information given to us from the outside world and to use this information to reason toward our own ends. The subordinate issues dealt with in knowledge representation and reasoning are propositional encoding, numerical cognition, mental imagery, media psychology, and dual-coding theories.

Language is another area researched commonly by cognitive psychologists. The acquisition of language, as well as the issues of language processing, grammar, linguistics, phonology, and phonetics, are the main areas of concern regarding language within the field of cognitive psychology. These studies often overlap with those of linguistics, but cognitive psychologists usually look more into the areas of language acquisition and processing than their counterparts.

Memory is likely to be the most commonly researched area of cognition within the field of cognitive psychology. Broadly, memory is the function of the brain by which pieces of information are stored, encoded, and retrieved when they are needed.

Age related memory loss is the most common issue concerning memory, as most of us have fair capabilities concerning memory that wane as we age. Autobiographical memory stores our recollections of our own past experiences, as its name would suggest. Childhood memory deals with childhood experiences. Constructive memory is a memory that erroneously constructs falsified recollections of past events. There is also a strong link between emotion and memory of all kinds that are researched by cognitive psychologists.

Episodic memory deals with past autobiographical events that can be recollected clearly, whereas eyewitness memory is just episodic memory that pertains to crimes or other dramatic events from a person's past. A false memory is merely an erroneous one, as its name would suggest. Flashbulb memories are short, incredibly detailed memories of past events. There are also long and short term memories and semantic memory, all of which we have gone over previously. The source-monitoring error occurs when the source of a memory is wrongfully attributed to some experience other than that which gave it birth. The psychological spacing effect can be used to our advantage when we space the repetition of our reviews of learned material in order to better remember said material. There are also many different types of memory biases that hinder our faculty of memory that will not be gone over here for the sake of brevity.

Perception is another area of great concern within cognitive psychology. Attention, object recognition, and pattern recognition is the three main areas of concern. Form perception is the most commonly studied form of perception within cognitive psychology. Psychophysics, a relatively new area of study, analyzes the relationship between the physical stimuli that we are met with and our perceptions and sensations related to them. Lastly, time sensation studies how we perceive and are affected by time.

Thinking is likely the broadest area of research within cognitive psychology. The term "thought" refers to the goal oriented flow of associations and ideas that can be driven towards reality oriented conclusions. A choice is a form of thought that follows a purposiveness presupposed by the chooser. This form of thought involved discerning the merits and demerits of options placed before us and choosing one or more of these options accordingly. The faculties of induction and acquisition used in concept formation are also forms of thought.

Decision making is the cognitive process of choosing one or more options presented to oneself, then initiating a course of action based on the choosing. Logic is inference studied systematically. A concise relation of logical support between the presuppositions made in the inference and the real conclusion has to be made in order for an inference to achieve validity. The psychology of reasoning is the scientific study of how people draw conclusions from information and make decisions based on those conclusions. Problem solving is simply the solving of issues we are faced with.

The main objective that cognitive psychologists aim to meet is the completion of models of the information processing that goes on inside a person's brain. Consciousness, memory, thinking, perception, attention, and language are the main areas of concern within this field. By completing these models, as the general idea goes, we can work with pre-established blueprints to determine how these processes are bound to take place in other individuals. The three main subcategories nested within this field are human experimental psychology (dealing primarily with issues concerning memory, attention, language, and problem solving), the approach of analogous computer information processing (including AI and computer simulations), and cognitive neuroscience (usually studying the effects of brain damage on cognition).

Around the 1950s a few developments in the psychological sciences necessitated the growth of cognitive psychology. These include but are not limited to the dissent from behaviorist psychology which placed much emphasis on external behaviors but none on the internal processes initiating these behaviors, development of newer, often more effective experimental methods, and new comparisons being drawn between the human mind and computer processing of information. Whether cognitive psychology answered the questions of the times surrounding these issues most effectively or not, behaviorism was becoming an extinct approach, driven out by its own antiquated methodology.

The rise of cognitive psychology was inversely proportional to the fall of some of the more erroneous approaches to psychology at the time. This field shook off the chaff of conditioned behavior and many psychoanalytic approaches of the time.

Behaviorists were typically averse to the study of the mind's internal processes because they believed that these processes could not be objectively observed and measured. Cognitive psychologists responded to this reluctance by observing and studying the mental processes of organisms, seeing doing so as an essential part of learning more about them. Mediational processes between stimulus and response within organisms were the first specific objects of study for cognitive psychologists, and remain paramount objects of study within the field to this day.

Cognitive psychologists did parallel behaviorists in that they employed controlled, objective, and scientific methods to pursue their ends. The only difference between the two groups here is that cognitive psychologists were using these methods to analyze the mental processes of organisms, whereas behaviorists were not.

Our brains are similar to computers in how they transform, store, and retrieve information (which should come as no surprise when considering that humans program computers). A clear sequence is shown in most models of information processing. The cognitive processes of attention and memory usually have the clearest of these sequences.

The analysis of stimuli is usually found within input processes. Storage processes within the brain can code and sometimes manipulate the perception of stimuli. Finally, output processes legislate our responses to stimuli.

In the late 1950s and early 1960s, the cognitive approach became the most widely accepted approach in the field of psychology, revolutionizing the way we perceive internal cognitive processes. The work of Piaget and Tolman is the main reason for this reality.

Tolman is considered by most today to be a soft behaviorist. His study of purposive behaviors in organisms, however, diverged from the behaviorist paradigm stating that learning was the product of the relationship between stimuli and responses. Tolman asserted to the contrary that learning stemmed from the relationships between stimuli amongst one another. The term he coined to refer to these relationships was "cognitive maps".

It was not until the arrival of the computer that cognitive psychology would gain the metaphor and terminology it needed to properly investigate the mind. This arrival gave psychologists the opportunity to draw analogies between the human mind and the processes of a computer, the latter being, on the whole, much more simple and easily understood. This analogy hearkens back to that one drawn by Plato in his Republic between the individual components of a state and the human mind. What more, this analogy also became the focal point of the Leibnitz-Searle argument. Essentially, a computer encodes information, changes it, stores it, uses it, and finally produces an output of some sort.

This computerized model of information processing was observed by cognitive psychologists who believed that the same or a similar model was used within the human brain. This approach is, however, rooted in a few key assumptions: that information from our external environment is processed by a series of processes (including perception, attention, memory, etc.), that transformation and alteration of these processes occur in systematic ways, that research is supposed to aim at specifying these processes and systems, and that computer information processing resembles that of humans.

The behaviorist approach offers us that we can observe and study the external (stimulus and response) processes that we are met with, but our observations under this approach are limited only to these external processes. The cognitive approach, to contrast, asserts that we can observe and study the internal processes going on within the mind. This approach studies the mediational relationships between stimulus/input and response/output.

The behaviorist approach works in a linear progression within the following frame: stimulus from the environment, a "black box" which cannot be studied, and response behavior. The cognitive approach follows a similar progression: input from the environment, a mediational process in the mental event, and output behavior. As we can see, aside from differences in verbiage, the main difference between these two progressions is found in their transient steps: while the behaviorist approach only offers us a black box of ignorance as to internal mental processes, the cognitive approach investigates the mediational processes occurring within mental events.

These mediational processes are so called because they are meant to go in between the stimulus and the response of the mental event. This response could include processes such as problem solving, attention, memory, perception, etc. Whatever they might be, these processes come about after the stimulus has been met and before the behavioral response is found.

The causal relationships between all of these mental processes in some instances beg teleological judgments regarding their parts. Here we see clear, linear paths of purposive behaviors following stimuli and subsequent mediational processes. Where the behaviorist model is said to lack here is in the knowledge of these intermediary mediational processes that go on within the mind. It is clear to us today that in order to understand behavioral psychology we must first understand these mediational processes. To do otherwise would be in many ways to put the cart before the horse.

It was Kohler's 1925 book *mentality of the apes* that started the popular split from the behaviorist model within the psychological sciences. In this book Kohler investigated the more insightful behaviors of animals, founding a little known field by the name of Gestalt psychology in the process. The terms input and output, so commonly used in cognitive psychology, were first introduced into the field in Norbert Wiener's 1948 book *Cybernetics: or control and communication in the animal and the machine.* Tolman's 1948 observations on cognitive maps done on rats in mazes were the first study to prove that animals have internal representations of behaviors.

It was *The magical number 7 plus or minus 2* of 1958 by George Miller that ultimately saw the birth of cognitive psychology. The general problem solver developed by Newell and Simon was the next great discovery within the field. In 1960, the Center for Cognitive Studies was finally founded by Miller and cognitive developmentalist Jerome Bruner. Ulric Neisser's 1967 publication of *"Cognitive psychology"* marks the definitive birth of the cognitive approach. Shiffrin and Atkinson's 1968 Multi Store model became the first processing model of memory. Today, at last, cognitive psychology is seen as a highly influential field throughout all areas of psychological study (biological, behaviorist, social, developmental, etc.).

A cognitive psychologist would be helpful to speak to for anyone who might be experiencing the following issues: a psychological issue that may need cognitive therapy methods to mitigate or exterminate, brain trauma that may need treatment, sensory and or perceptual issues, a speech or language disorder (more types of therapy would be needed in this case, with cognitive methods being supplementary), memory related problems such as Alzheimer's disease, dementia, or memory loss, or learning disabilities.

In essence, nearly anyone who has or is experiencing issues concerning mental processes will necessarily benefit from cognitive psychological therapy. Many feel that cognitive psychology is an erudite and impractical field of study that has much more utility within the classroom than without, but everyone has mental processes, so everyone can benefit from this area of research. Having a cognitive psychologist working for and with us will give us a more objective, scientific perspective on the mental processes we have that we may not be aware of or may be interpreting unscientifically.

One of the most stealthy adversaries of our own wellbeing is negative thinking patterns. These thinking patterns are so destructive because we usually cannot tell just how distorted they are, which enables them to legislate our thought processes without our conscious awareness. Having another perspective on our own internal mental processes is arguably the only surefire way to keep these negative patterns from controlling the rest of our minds. Negative ruminations often lead to increased stress, self-sabotaging, pessimism, and even learned helplessness after a while is we are not careful.

Once these negative thinking patterns have taken their hold over our psyches they cannot necessarily be removed. Our best option is to then replace these patterns with better, more optimistic and rational ones. For instance, a schema that is telling a person repeatedly things like "you are not worthy" or "you will never meet the standards" should be responded to with one that tells him or her things like "you have intrinsic worth" or "these standards are your own". The negative thinking patterns, as well as the rational responses to their interjections, are indeterminate and depend on the individual. All the same, the basic goal is to replace the thoughts that do not assist us or do not push us forward as individuals with ones that do. Here some self therapy could be utilized. Whenever we have a thought or a series of thoughts that our executive minds do not agree with, we should record and analyze these thoughts, editing them and replacing them with healthier, more rational ones. Doing so will change our modes of thinking and enable us to become more rational, intrinsically motivated people.

Cognitive psychology could be considered the final purpose of psychology, the one to which all other subfields are subordinate. Everything that we know of, we know of because of our ability to cognize. Without analyzing our mental processes we are leaving ourselves in the dark as to what is really going on in and outside of us.

Chapter six: Modes of persuasion

We come at last to what is likely the most useful portion of our book. Modes of persuasion, also known as rhetorical appeals or ethical strategies, are rhetorical devices used to classify a speaker's appeal to his or her audience. These modes are called Eros, pathos, logos, and Kairos. Aristotle considered persuasion to be merely a form of demonstration, as we are most fully persuaded by the things that we perceive as having been demonstrated. It could logically follow that the more or less we demonstrate something, the more or fewer others will be persuaded of it within proportion.

There are three main kinds of spoken word persuasion: persuasion due to a perceived credibility of the speaker at the time of the speech, persuasion of the hearers due to their own emotions, and persuasion achieved through speech when truth or apparent truth is arrived at by arguments suited to the case in question.

Ethos is broadly defined as either the appeal to authority or to the speaker's credibility. In order to bolster ethos a speaker must convince the audience of his or her own credibility, often appealing to other sources of authority in the process. People employ various means of doing this, including but not limited to being or becoming a notable figure in the field in question, such as a professor, doctor, or expert, learning and demonstrating a mastery of the vernacular of the field in question, and introducing or producing proven experts in the field.

Without these broad criteria met, a speaker will generally have trouble gaining and fostering a sense of credibility or ethos.

Without being an expert in the field in which he or she is speaking on, or without the necessary vocabulary and or appeal to other sources of authority, a speaker will typically lose any sense of credibility in the eyes of his or her audience, usually causing the individual to lose his or her sense of intrinsic credibility, thus starting a causal loop of the loss of overall credibility and potency as a speaker.

Ethos could be considered persuasion by character or credibility. Trustworthiness is usually the most important trait that a person can display in order to foster ethos. We tend to see those who are more trustworthy as also being more credible, as while we may not know what they are going to tell us, we are more assured that it is going to be the truth. It would necessarily follow here that in order for someone to gain ethos, he or she must become more trustable. Aristotle offers us three explicit qualities that a person must display in order to become a more trustworthy individual: good sense, good moral character, and a good will.

Good sense is found only in rational and responsible thinkers. We tend to trust those with good sense much more than we do others. Those with good sense are almost always calm, cool, and collected in times of stress and confusion. Those people are usually seen as trusted and reliable professionals within their fields of work. Good sense is associated with trustworthiness because those who have it are impelled more by logic and rationality than others without it are. With good sense, a speaker is also able to read a crowd better and to deliver messages that are more grounded in reality.

Good moral judgment was another area in which Aristotle placed lots of emphases. It is commonly said that character is what we do when no one is looking. The same is true for morality. Aristotle thought that having this sense of moral judgment was crucial to developing the art of persuasion.

Finally, good will is the state in which a person truly has our own best interests in mind. Without this will there is no clear direction within a person's mind as to where things should go or even how they should ideally be. If a speaker shows no knowledge or regard for the interests of the whole that he or she is speaking to then rapport will never be built. While a person's ethos is probably less affected by a lack of good will than by a lack of any of the other two goods, people are still put off by this absence because they will not be sure whether or not the speaker is truly on their side. It is only, as Aristotle asserts, with these three qualities that a person can be more trustworthy and gain ethos.

Pathos may be a more powerful mode of persuasion because it is dependent on a speaker's ability to appeal to the emotions of the audience. From this root word the words empathy, pathetic, and sympathy are formed. Using the common tactics of metaphor, simile, and overall passionate delivery pathos can be gained by the speaker. Often, even simple claims asserting things to be unjust are enough to appeal to the emotions of speakers. This mode of persuasion is incredibly effective when used with others but usually falls apart when used as a standalone. There are one main criterion that a speaker needs to meet in order to gain pathos though; he or she needs to deliver a message that is in agreement with some underlying values of the readers or listeners.

To gain pathos, a speaker may home in on any emotions he or she feels to be of use to tap into. These include happiness and optimism, but also include more negative emotions such as fear and anxiety. Whatever the emotions might be, a speaker with a sensitivity to the audience's emotions gains rapport with ease by speaking to people about what they find most salient.

Our adoption of beliefs and viewpoints is largely dependent upon our immediate emotions. A good speaker not only knows how to exalt certain emotions but also how to eliminate certain others. In order to get people angry about a cause, a good speaker will explain the qualms behind not following that cause. Likewise, if a crowd of people is angry about gas prices, a good speaker will calm them down and give them the assurance that they will continue to be able to get around. A persuasive person keeps in mind what others are concerned about, and offers them solutions to their problems.

When used within speeches and writings, pathos is often played on the audience's imagination and aspirations regarding future events. Persuasive thinkers are not only able to predict and speak to present emotions but are also able to convey some sort of an image of what the future could be like under their vision. Without this emphasis placed on the teleological purposiveness of what the persuader is thinking, the persuaded is left with no determinative course of action to follow and is thus destined to become unpersuaded.

While a certain amount of ethos has to be secured in order for a speaker to be listened to, this ethos is often downplayed and is put in a role subordinate to pathos. When pathos is the main mode used we often start to see less control within speech and writing and more appeal to the base and often irrational emotions. William Cullen Bryant saw this as an alright happening, claiming that anyone speaking out of righteousness will give to the world an offering that will outweigh any amount of errors that they bring with it.

Aristotle offers us some of the basic dualities of emotion in book 2 of his *rhetoric:*

Anger vs. calm

People tend to get angry when we show contempt towards, shame, or act spitefully against them. Contempt is here defined as the treating of things or people that others value as unimportant. Acting with spite is keeping others from getting what they want just to harm them. Shame is given when we discredit others in some way. Doing the opposite of these things, such as leaving things and people in their own value, holding others in esteem, and letting others have what they want, will keep people calm.

Friendship vs. hatred

It is those who act without selfishness in order to achieve what is best for us who we choose to be friends with. We show hatred towards those who are either selfish or who work towards harmful ends. Contingents are only formed among people who have common interests in mind. We divide our world into those who work with us (friends) and those who do not (foes).

Fear vs. confidence

We are fearful only of the things that we perceive to be able to bring us harm or suffering. When we do not perceive these dangers to exist, or have means of combating them, we instead feel confident. The confidence deriving from our perceived ability to combat danger is the more reliable of the two because any confidence derived from a lack of danger intimates danger in the future.

Shame vs. shameless

We feel shame when we have been discredited for displaying what Aristotle called moral badness, such as being cowardly, arrogant, avaricious, or mean. We feel shameless when we are either indifferent to or contemptible of other's perceptions of our moral badness. Shame is the concept of moral badness (real or perceived) attached to the concept of self-consciousness. Shamelessness is this concept divorced from self-consciousness.

Kind vs. unkind

We are perceived as being kind when we help others for their own sake. We are perceived as unkind when we either neglect to help others or help them merely for our own sake. Kindness is found in those who keep the interests of those who they are helping in mind. Unkindness is found in those who either do not help others or who do so for their own gains.

Pity vs. indignation

We feel pity for those who are suffering in ways and calibers that we perceive to be unproportionally to aptness. On the other hand, we feel indignation when we see others doing well and feel that they do not deserve it. Pity is felt when we see someone suffer more than is necessary, while indignation is felt when we see someone get more than their character is deserving of, or so we think.

Envy vs. emulation

Envy is felt when we see another who we consider our equal come across a good fortune. This is more keenly felt when we feel that we are entitled to the same good fortune or when we no longer see ourselves as equal to that person as a result of the fortunate circumstances. Envy stems from selfishness in that it does not offer that we may live vicariously through the other individual. We are most envious of those who we perceive to be more fortunate than us because every person wants to believe that he or she is equal to all others.

Emulation is felt when we see another who has good fortune and feel that we can achieve a similar fortune. Here we have the same stimuli as that which causes envy, but our mediational response is more constructive and positive. Aristotle considered, like most would, emulation to be the better of these two feelings because while envious people often wish the more fortunate person to have less, emulative people merely strive to achieve more. Envy is the perception of inequality with the concept of dislike towards those with more, while emulation is the same perception with the concept of self efficacy.

The concept of a human being necessarily includes that of emotion. Emotions are never right or wrong, they are only rational or irrational. Sometimes, for instance, fear and anger are the only rational responses to external realities, while at other times serenity and happiness are called for. A good persuader knows the ins and outs of the emotions of others, whether they be rational or irrational. With this knowledge, a persuader can exalt the emotions he or she wants to in other individuals, and curtail all others.

Logos is, broadly, an appeal to logic. The term logic actually derives from this one. There is generally some sort of thesis that a speaker is trying to communicate when speaking. Logic, in part, refers to the facts and figures supporting these theses, in this case. Having logos tends to beget greater ethos for a speaker because the information makes the speaker seem more knowledgeable to his or her listener(s). While logos can be incredibly useful, it can also be harmful and misleading, depending on the content of the information and its relationship with the subject at hand. Often, mis contextualized, falsified, and or inaccurate information leads listeners astray, causing them to leave the speaker and causing the speaker to lose ethos.

Aristotle tells us of three main methods of logical persuasion:

Deductive argument

In its initial stage, a sound, logical argument will put forth a series of axiomatic premises. These statements are perceived to be either true or false. From these premises, we can lead ourselves to conclusions. If a conclusion were said to be true given that all of its axiomatic premises were also said to be true then the argument would be considered valid. If all of these premises are true and the argument is said to be valid then it is also, by definition, sound. These arguments are what is known as deductive arguments. Within these arguments, the notions of validity and soundness are defined and observed from premises to conclusions. These are good arguments because they use easily intelligible logic throughout their courses.

Inductive argument

If from our initial premises, we instead find conclusions that are not necessarily but likely to be true then we are making inductive arguments. These arguments exist with the concept of uncertainty and some amount of guesswork. The strength or weakness of an inductive argument is found only in the likelihood of its conclusions to follow its premises. A cogent inductive argument is one in which all of its premises are, in fact, found to be true.

Abductive argument

An abductive argument is arrived at when we collect a set of data and then proceed to formulate a conclusion based on that data. This conclusion should always explain the data set in question. Like deductive arguments, the validity and soundness of these arguments are dependent upon the truth behind the conclusions.

Finally, Kairos refers to time and place. This mode is often used to instill a sense of urgency within the minds of the listeners, urging them to act on events as they happen.

In addition to the Aristotelian modes of persuasion, there are also numerous contemporary methods that could be used to our advantage. Though the Aristotelian modes are evergreen in their applicability, people are always coming up with new ways to persuade others, ways that are usually meant to appeal more to the people of the time.

Mimicry is one of the most surefire methods of persuasion. We tend to be much more receptive to messages when they are delivered by people who speak, think, and act as we do. Using mimicry will almost invariably boost rapport, make others like us more, and make us seem more agreeable all around. When trying to persuade others we should always take note of how they are acting and speaking, and mirror these characteristics as much as possible in order to foster a sense of kinship with us in their minds. This will put us on the same ground as them, so to speak, ensuring them that we share common interests with them and are willing to work with them to pursue these interests.

The Ellsberg Paradox was discovered in 1961 in a series of experiments conducted by Daniel Ellsberg. In these experiments, participants were told that they needed to choose between two urns to draw a ball from, the first containing 100 red and black balls with no certain proportion between the two colors, the second with exactly 50 red balls and 50 black ones. There reward was $100 if they chose the correct color, $0 if they did not. The vast majority of subjects drew from the second urn with the determinate proportion of colors.

These experiments show that we are naturally prone to avoid risk and uncertainty whenever possible. While we may benefit more from taking bets on uncertainties at times, it remains our natural proclivity to stick to certain, concise probabilities wherever we find them, even when our payoffs are shown to be less for doing so.

Social influence, or social proof, refers to our being affected by the thoughts, emotions, and behaviors of others. We are impressed upon by this sort of influence largely unconsciously, which is why it is often difficult to discern what we are doing out of our own interests from what we are doing as a result of this influence. Here the question asserts itself: to what extent are we merely the products of those around us?

Most people can be analyzed as a collection of their immediate social influences.

No matter how independently minded we happen to be, we do crave external validation in order to make our thinking patterns seem "normal" to us. The people who we most admire end up being the highest authorities as to how we should think, feel, and behave, whether we like or realize it or not.

Reciprocity is another assistant of persuasion. When we receive things from others, whatever they might be, we usually feel the urge to reciprocate. When we feel this urge it compels us to appease the other, making us much more likely to be persuaded by the individual. When we give others things we are not only compelling them to reciprocate but are also making them much more likely to work with us in the future. People need an incentive of some sort in order to work towards our ends. There must be some way in which a person can gain from working with us. By doing favors and giving others things we are giving them this incentive, and urging them to reciprocate and do the same for us. We are, however, affected by experiences in an inverse proportion to their temporal distances from us, so when we do things for other people they will usually feel more compelled to reciprocate right afterwards, and this compulsion will only wane with the passage of time.

The hot hand fallacy is another phenomenon that we can use to our advantage. This is a fallacy by which people lead themselves to believe that since they happen to be finding immediate successes they will continue to do so indefinitely. While success does often beget success, life is ultimately chaotic and random and vicissitudes tend to present themselves when we least expect them to. The fallacy's modus operandi is found within the (presumptively false) perception of control that it gives us.

People are much likely to be persuaded of their future successes when they are experiencing successes. Again, the closer an experience is to us temporally, the more we are affected by it. This affection extends to our perceptions, which in this case implies that more recent successes will cause us to believe that we will have better futures. In order to persuade someone by taking advantage of this fallacy, we should lead them to believe that they are currently experiencing success, and continue to press that things are only looking up for them.

A sense of commitment and consistency will cause us to stick with the things that we choose, whatever these things might be. Whatever choices we happen to make in life, it is within our nature to stick to these choices until they show themselves to be faulty ones, if they ever do so. Along these veins that we carve for ourselves, we will travel until the change becomes necessary.

If we are trying to persuade others, we can use their sense of commitment to our advantage by first getting them to agree to smaller things, and eventually working them into bigger and bigger commitments as time goes on. People are put off by being granted too much responsibility at once. We instead prefer to ease ourselves into things by taking time to transition into them. Persuasion is, in part, a game of small asks, each one building on top of the last, leading to the greater and greater commitment between parties.

When making a decision we tend to rely all too heavily on the first pieces of information that we come across. This tendency is called anchoring and it is considered fallacious because it causes us to graze over other useful pieces of information that could help us with our decision making.

Once an anchor has been set, a bias towards its idea is also set. From this, it would necessarily follow that people are much more likely to be persuaded of something when an initial anchoring towards it has been made. If we are trying to convince someone to make a certain decision then we are going to need to give them some initial piece of information from which they can base their further decisions.

Next, simply liking another person makes us much more receptive to them. One of the greatest proponents of persuasiveness is simple likability. We are never positively influenced by those we do not like, regardless of their character. We seek to squash these people's opinions whenever we come across them and are never persuaded by the things they say as a result. In order to get a person on our side, we have to treat them in a way that causes them to like us, because without their doing so no sense of comradery can be fostered, and without any sense of comradery we will never be able to persuade them of anything.

Being friendly with others is probably the best way to get them to like us. Remembering to smile and remaining light hearted around others will make people feel more comfortable around us, opening up the door to more friendly and amiable conversations.

Sensory words should always be taken note of when trying to convince others. These words are some of the most powerful ones that we use, and people are likely more affected by these words than by any others. Words with connotations to sensory stimuli that people find agreeable can be used to convince people often without their knowing. These words are more than just words to those who hear them, they are real, tangible experiences associated with sensory experiences, so using these words wisely can have a surprisingly powerful effect on the decision making processes of those who hear them.

We also have a bias towards authority. The thoughts and opinions of authority figures are often regarded as much more valuable than they really are. We are socialized from a young age to respect authority figures and take what they say seriously. This is why the things these people say are listened to more than the things other people say. Here is where ethos remains important. In order to be listened to, not to mention to be persuasive, we have to convince our audience that we are some sort of authority on what we are talking about.

The Ikea effect is a phenomenon by which people tend to value things that they have assembled more highly than things that have come to them preassembled. We take pride in whatever it is that we produce, and consider these products to be better and more valuable than those of any others. Giving people a sense of participation in whatever it is that we are proposing to them will make them much more receptive to our ideas because they will feel as though they are a part of something that gives them a say.

People like to have options and to feel as though they are in control of what options they pursue. When we make our premises and arguments seem more customizable to others, they will identify more with what we are saying because we are encouraging something of a negotiated dialogue to take place between ourselves and them. This sense of oneness can make people much more likely to follow us wherever we decide to go intellectually.

Chapter seven: Controlling emotions

The workplace tends to be one of the most difficult places to control emotions. No matter how hard you try, those difficult days are always bound to come up. In your personal life, your reactions to stressful situations are much freer, but in the workplace, your reactions are subject to the scrutiny of your coworkers. Any emotional outbursts while working cannot only damage your professional reputation and productivity, but they can even get you fired.

Under normal circumstances, it is usually easy to maintain composure in the workplace, but under more stressful circumstances, such as staff layoffs, budget cuts, and department changes, staying calm can prove difficult, if not impossible. Under these circumstances, however, it becomes even more important to keep your temper, as bosses typically consider the demeanor of their employees when deciding who gets laid off. You have complete freedom and how you react to certain situations, but that freedom comes with responsibility, especially in the workplace.

It may seem easy to decide how you're going to react in certain situations with hindsight, but it is always advisable to explore techniques in dealing with these situations and emotions. Here we will discuss many negative emotions associated with employment, as well as many methods of coping with these emotions.

The most commonly reported negative emotions among workers are as follows:

Worry/ nervousness, frustration/ irritation, dislike, anger/ aggravation, disappointment/ unhappiness

And now we will get into some strategies in dealing with these unhealthy emotions.

Worry/ nervousness

These are two of the most unpleasant and unhealthy emotions on the spectrum, and, unfortunately for workers, these two plague virtually every workplace. This anxiety can stem from a number of sources: fear of getting laid off, social problems, low salaries, large workload, etc., And be compounded with problems at home, or with family or friends by many. A small amount of stress can be a productive thing, but once it becomes chronic anxiety, health problems start to occur. Here are some tips on how to avoid excessive anxiety:

Break cycles of worry
Do not Surround yourself with anxiety. If you can foresee needless anxiety stemming from a situation or a conversation, avoid that anxiety. Try to minimize the number of anxiety inducing things that you have to deal with.

Try deep breathing exercises
These help primarily to slow down your breathing and heart rate. There are all sorts of different deep breathing exercises that you can learn about on the internet. For one, there is cyclical breathing, with in breaths for 4 seconds followed by holding for 4 seconds, and then out breaths for 4 seconds followed by holding for 4 seconds. When doing these exercises, it is important to focus on your breathing and nothing else. In addition to these exercises, there are other

physical relaxation exercises that will help reduce workplace stress, including progressive muscle relaxation.

Focus on improving the situation
Whatever it is worrying you in regards to work, brainstorming solutions and making attempts at them will help reduce your anxiety greatly. Doing these things will also make you a more valuable asset to your company.

Journal your worries down
Simply writing down the things that bother you will do a lot to alleviate the anxiety surrounding them. This technique also helps to curtail sleep problems and nightmares, as worries that we write down during the day don't typically bother us by night. Once these are written down, you can then schedule times to deal with these issues. Before that time comes, let these issues leave you and go about your day. When that time comes, make sure to perform proper risk analysis before putting any plans into place.

Worry and nervousness can decrease self-confidence and lead to health complications. it is always important to trail these negative emotions away and remain confident and secure.

Frustration/irritation

Frustration is more often than not caused by the feeling of being trapped or stuck at a point which you want to get out of, but cannot. This feeling can be caused by a number of things, especially at work. A colleague blocking a project of yours, a boss too disorganized to catch a meeting on time, or a phone call held out longer than necessary are just a few examples that come to mind. Frustration, whatever its causes, should always be dealt with quickly because when it is not it can accumulate into anger and other even more negative emotions.

There are, however, many ways of dealing with this awful emotion, a few of which are listed below:

Stopping to evaluate
The best thing to do when feelings of frustration arise is to stop what you are doing and take time to evaluate them. Writing your frustrations down in this stage can help very much. After this is done, think of some positive aspects of your current situation. This will improve your mood and reduce further frustration.

Look for positive things
Again, finding silver linings in a frustrating situation will make you see the events unfolding in a new light. This change in your thinking will improve your mood, among other things. If it is a person who is causing you frustration than keep in mind that it is probably not personal, and if it is an event or situation, than it can probably be solved. Try to move on from this step as much as possible.

Recall the last time you felt frustrated
If you can remember the last thing that you were frustrated about than you can probably remember how that thing eventually resolved itself. Looking at things with hindsight, they always work out fine. You can also probably recall that your feelings of frustration did not do much to help you in that last situation, so to assume that they are helping you this time around would not be very prudent. Perspective is everything, and so many issues lose so much of their stature when seen through different angles.

Dislike

Dislike for certain coworkers is inevitable, and when it pops up, it seldom goes away. We all have to work with people who we dislike at one point or another, so when these people arrive, it is important to take steps towards dealing with them responsibly. Some of the best things that you can do in these situations are to:

Show respect
You are never obligated to get along with everyone you work with, but you are, in many ways, obligated to show them all respect. When these situations arise, pride and ego are two things which you should set aside, even if the other party(s) are not willing to. This will allow you to come out of the experience with your dignity intact, whatever the outcomes may be.

Be assertive
If a coworker is rude or unprofessional with you, do not be afraid to tell them so. If you do so with certainty and fairness, they might be inclined to change some of their attitudes and behaviors in the future.

Anger/aggravation

Anger is arguably the most destructive emotion contained in a human. This is especially true when the anger is out of control in the workplace. It is also an emotion which most of us do not handle very well. As far as work is concerned, there is typically very little room for anger, which is problematic because much of it then gets taken home with us. Controlling this emotion is one of the most important steps in keeping any given job, especially for those who have difficulties with this. Some tips in dealing with this emotion are listed below:

Watch for the early signs of anger
No one else can detect when your anger is building up quite like you can, so detecting it early is your own responsibility. As was mentioned before, you decide how to react to situations, so if you react in anger, no one holds accountability for that happening.

When anger arises, take a break from what you are doing
When you start to get angry, closing your eyes and trying the aforementioned deep breathing exercises can help you hugely. These actions will do a lot to interrupt your angry thoughts and help to put your mind back on a more positive, relaxed pathway, reducing irrational statements and decisions made.

Picture yourself when you get angry
Imagining how you look and behave will usually give you some well needed perspective on the situation at hand. For example, if you have the urge to shout at a coworker, think about what you would look like doing so: flustered, mean, and demanding. With that imagery in mind, it is easy to see that you would not be a good coworker in making that decision.

Disappointment/unhappiness

Disappointment and unhappiness are two of the more pullulated emotions in modern workplaces. These two are almost equal to anger in their unhealthiness, in fact, unhappiness may be more unhealthy. These can also have detrimental impacts on your productivity, as they can leave you feeling exhausted and drained, and also less inclined to take risks in the future. Here are some steps that can be taken to curtail the effects of these awful emotions.

Consider your mindset
Try to always keep in mind that things will not always go your way. If they did, then life would become prosaic and meaningless. It is, sometimes, the adversity and the suffering that give life its meat. Do not try to avoid these things, the answer to these problems lies within the willingness to confront them.

Set and adjust your goals
Disappointment can often stem from neglecting to reach a goal. This rarely means, however, that the goal is no longer reachable though. It is natural to feel disappointment in these situations, but you must always find the willpower to pick yourself back up. You could, for example, keep your goal, but just make a small change. Anything that will help you to get past the disappointments that you face.

Record your thoughts
One method for dealing with negative emotions is to write them down. When you feel unhappy or disappointed, try writing down what is bothering you, and be specific about your concerns. Is it your job that is bothering you? A coworker? Do you have too heavy of a workload? Writing these concerns down will help you to single out what exactly is bothering you and how you can improve on these areas of concern. Remember that you always have more powers than you think in improving a situation.

Remember to smile
Forcing a smile onto your face can actually make you feel happier and relieve stress. In addition, this activity also

releases the neurotransmitters dopamine, endorphins, and serotonin, which all lower heart rate and blood pressure. The endorphins released also act as natural painkillers and the serotonin acts as a natural antidepressant. Smiling will also make you look more attractive to those around you, further bettering the relationships you have with your coworkers.

Now that the main emotions that have adverse effects on most workers have been covered, let's take a look at some more strategies of dealing with these:

Compartmentalize your stressors

Try to keep stress and baggage from work and home in those respective places. You can use mental techniques, such as imagining the stressors locked away in a box for the time being. If you do not try to compartmentalize these issues, then waters will get very muddied up in your personal life and things will become very complicated.

Identify your own self talk

Relay to yourself what you tell yourself. By doing this, you may find yourself repeating thoughts and phrases to yourself that are not necessarily true or helpful. Try to identify your own thoughts that may be misleading or based on thinking errors. Doing this will help you move on from some of your worse points and attitudes into a more productive and expansive mindset.

Identify and accept your emotion

There is virtually nothing you can do to control an emotion that you are not even willing to come to terms with having. It is like denying the existence of a spider right in front of your eyes, the spider will just get bigger and bigger until it is all that you can see. In identifying what emotion(s) you are having and accepting that they are a natural part of life, you are taking lots of power away from them. In doing this, you are also becoming a greater solver of your own problems.

Affirm your rights

There are many places in life, work especially, where you are bound to feel like you have no rights and no control over what happens to you. By identifying your rights and your powers, you are giving yourself some perspective on the things that are in and out of your control. After taking some time to do this, you may find that you are much more powerful than you think you are. This will improve your mood and your self-confidence to affirm these rights that you have.
Communicate strategically

Anyone can drone on about the things that they do not like, but it takes skill and grit to actually get things done to fix all their problems. When you are trying to communicate with others, especially disagreements, It is always important to be precise in your language. This will allow you to communicate your qualms more effectively, and it will also decrease the chance of having misunderstandings and heated arguments. When trying to get a point across, try to come into the situation with some idea of what you want to get accomplished and your probability of having a productive conversation will increase dramatically. If others reply emotionally, let them vent and be understanding. You may learn more from them than they will from you. Ask for more details as well and the two of you will probably come closer to an understanding because of it.

Be objective

Try to look at whatever is bothering you from both analytic and synthetic approaches. An analytic approach will help you understand the one issue more in depth and with more clarity, while a synthetic approach will help you understand the issue within the class of all of your possible issues. It is important to look into things with depth and focus, but seeing things as parts of your whole understanding will help you to make connections and find out why these certain things bother you through free associations.

Emotions are never right or wrong, they are only felt. There is no shame in feeling emotions unless of course, the emotion is a shame. Emotions will always come and go and are always wiser than the ego. Each one of us, however, has freewill in how we react to life's vicissitudes. Controlling emotions is not always easy, in fact, sometimes it becomes nearly impossible. But this skill is just like any other in that it can be improved with practice and diligence.

Chapter eight: Social engineering and leadership

The importance of social engineering and leadership are often underestimated by contemporary thinkers. Most people are so absorbed in manipulating and taking down hierarchical structures that they neglect to figure out how to manifest themselves within these structures. Whether you have a proclivity towards leadership or not, it still remains important to have a working knowledge of leadership and how it works among groups of people.

Leaders, above all else, help themselves and others in making steps towards doing the right things. In doing this they build an inspiring vision, set direction, and create new possibilities. Leadership is, in part, about mapping out the route to your team's successful future. It is challenging, but also exciting, dynamic, and inspiring. Setting the direction of the pack is not the only responsibility of a leader though. They are also obligated to guide their people in these directions in a smooth and efficient way. This may be the more challenging skill which takes more time to develop.

This chapter and its tips on the process of leadership will be based on the 'transformational model' of leadership proposed by James MacGregor Burns and further developed by Bernard Bass. This model more so focuses on bringing about change through visionary leadership than the normative managerial processes designed to maintain the current performance of given groups.

An overview of leadership

The following are a few traits of an effective leader:

1. Succeeds in creating an inspiring vision of the future
2. Inspires and motivates people to engage with that vision
3. Manages the delivery of the vision
4. Builds and coaches a team, so that it becomes more effective in meeting the vision

Effective leadership requires all of these traits working together with one another. Next, it would be helpful to explore each one of these elements in greater detail.

Succeeds in creating an inspiring vision of the future

In the workforce, a vision that a boss prognosticates needs to be a convincing, realistic, and attractive depiction of the situation that you want to be in in the future. This vision should set priorities, provide direction and a marker to people to assure that all are able to see whether or not the goals set forth have been achieved.

To create a reliable vision, leaders must first assess and analyses their current situation to get an understanding of where to go. Some steps that are appropriate to take in this stage are considering the evolution of their industry in the future, considering the behaviors of their competitors, and how to innovate successfully to shape their business for competition in the future marketplace. The next step is to undergo some scenario analysis to assess the validity of their vision.

Leadership is, therefore, proactive rather than reactive; looking ahead, problem solving, and constantly evolving.

Once a leader's vision has been developed, it is necessary to sell the vision. In order to do this, he or she has to make the vision compelling and convincing. A compelling vision allows people to understand, embrace, see, and feel it. Effective leaders can communicate their visions effectively and clearly. They are able to speak about their visions in ways that people can relate to and they inform people in an inspired way. This makes people more receptive of their ideas and more inclined to follow what they have to say.

Shared values and vision creation are two major components of leadership. Those who can develop skills in these two areas are more likely to succeed in leadership roles.

Inspires and motivates people to engage with that vision

The foundation of leadership is a compelling vision. This vision is only met, however, by a leader's ability to inspire and motivate his or her followers. At the beginning of most projects, it is easier to stay enthusiastic, which in turn makes it easier to win support for it than in other stages of the project. After the initial enthusiasm fades is when it becomes more difficult to maintain an inspiring vision moving forward. People change along with their attitudes and working methods, as well as their goals. Good leadership requires recognizing this phenomenon and working hard throughout a given project to be cognizant of others' needs, hopes, and desires while meeting the vision at hand. It is a juggling act of altruism and pragmatism that helps wherever it goes.

One means of linking effort, motivation, and outcome is known as expectancy theory. This place is an emphasis on leaders linking two main expectations that their followers have. These are listed below:

The expectation of hard work leading to good results.
And
The expectation of good results leading to incentives or rewards.

People with these expectations foresee both intrinsic and extrinsic rewards and therefore work harder to achieve success.

One other approach includes repeatedly restating the vision with added emphasis on its rewards and communicating the vision in a more effective and attractive way.

Expert power is one of the most helpful things that a leader can have. People are more inclined to admire and believe in leaders with this because they are seen as experts at what they do. Expertise comes with credibility, respect, and prestige. This also potentially gives people a right and even an obligation to lead others. Having and displaying competence gives leaders a much easier time motivating and inspiring their followers.

Natural Charisma and appeal can also serve as conduits for a leader's motivation of and influence over people, as well as other sources of power. These other sources of power include the ability to assign tasks to people and to pay bonuses.

Managing the delivery of the vision

This area of leadership applies more to management than any of these other tips.

Leaders always need to make sure that they are properly managing the work necessary for delivering their vision. This can be done by either themselves, a manager, or a team of managers delegated by the leader to deliver the vision of the leader.

In order to achieve this, team members need to meet their performance goals linked to the company's vision. Some means of seeing that this is done are KPIs (key performance indicators), performance management, and project management. One other way of ensuring that the vision is being met is a management style called management by wandering around (MBWA). This style ensures that all the steps that need to be taken are taken in meeting any given goals.

Another trait of an effective leader is the ability to manage change well. Leadership is, after all, constant evolution and adjusting to work's vicissitudes. Managing changes smoothly and efficiently ensures that all goals will be met and obstacles overcome throughout the course of realizing the leader's vision. This can only be done, however, with the backing and support of the people behind the leader.

Building and coaching a team to achieve the vision

Some of the more crucial activities carried out by transformational leaders are individual and team development. Without these, there would be nothing for the leader to lead. The first step in developing a team that a leader has to take is to come to understand team dynamics. There are several popular and well-established models that can describe these to leaders, including Belbin's team roles approach, and the forming, storming, norming, performing, and adjourning theory of Bruce Tuckman. A more in depth analysis of this theory is featured below:

Forming
The forming step involves a team coming together at the beginning of a venture to figure the goals of the group out and how to go about accomplishing these. Members tend to be impersonal and polite during this period as everyone is still getting oriented within the team.

Storming
The storming phase is a bit more selective and critical. In this phase, the leadership may be questioned along with group members ideas. This is very much a culling-off phase of the process as many of the group's members will feel overwhelmed and disconcerted by the turbulence and criticism. Some of them who do not leave after this stage give up on the goal at hand as well. And some just simply do not want to do what is asked of them.

Norming
Norming is the step at which the group comes together to agree on a singular plan for achieving the common goal. In this stage, members of the group are encouraged to yield their ideas for the betterment of the group and they also come to know and understand each other better, building stronger relationships. It is working towards a common goal that brings the team members together.

Performing

By the performing stage of the process, the group members are able to work towards accomplishing the goal without very much outside supervision or input. They also come to understand each other's needs better and how to work with one another to accomplish the goal at hand.

Adjourning
In the adjourning stage, the opportunity to reflect on unsuccessful and successful outcomes comes about. Members of the group can use these outcomes to gage what they should do when working on future tasks. This will help smooth out the process of meeting a goal in the future.

The next time you find yourself working in a group on a certain task, monitor the group's progress through these stages. Group members tend to move through these stages in all sorts of different orders. They actually rarely happen in the order listed above. If, however, team members are aware of the steps that they are moving through-which they usually are not- then they can typically work through these steps much more efficiently and effectively. Walking yourself through these steps listed above will help you navigate the happenings of your workplace better in the future.

A competent leader always does his or her best to ensure that team members are equipped with all the abilities and skills necessary to do their jobs and achieve the overarching vision. In order to do this, it is necessary to give and receive feedback on a day to day basis, as well as to train and coach team members on a regular basis as well. These steps will improve individual and team performances dramatically.

Good leaders lead, but great leaders lead and find leadership potential. When leading a team, it is always helpful to find leadership abilities on others, whatever their current positions may be. This paves the way for not only differentiation in hierarchical status, but also for further development beyond the leader's influence or even stay. It can also give a leader a surprisingly helpful example in other competent workers.

The terms 'leader' and 'leadership' are often misused to describe people who are actually in managerial positions. These people are often highly skilled and have great work-ethics, but that does not necessarily make them great leaders.

Workplaces are all too often hoisted up on people who others consider to be leaders but are actually managers. These managers often do not provide any aspirations or even long-term goals for their team members, which is fine in the short term, but eventually leads to feelings of meaninglessness and even resentment.

The next discussion points that should be delved into would have to be group dynamics and social engineering. These are important realms to know about when entering a new workplace, or any given social setting for that matter. Here we will look into what group dynamics are and what you need to know about them in order to master them.

Group dynamics, whether ignored by participants or not, play a major role in any culture, organization, or unit. People with differing ideas and perspectives make these groups up. It is very rare that all people and their ideologies are homogeneous within any given group. It is, in fact, also dangerous. Leaders are looked up to within these groups maintain the unity of purpose and cohesiveness of the unit. The cultural bonds within these units must be developed more at certain times than in others. Once these bonds are developed, the further effort has to be put in to nurture them.

Dysfunction within these groups occurs with alienation among specific members. When a member feels ostracized, there is very little keeping him or her from acting out in unpredictable ways. This is bound to come up at times and when it does the leader can struggle to remain objective as the structure of the cohesive unit starts to fall apart. These are usually the worst periods of chaos in the histories of groups. It is these periods, however, that separate good leaders from bad ones.

At all times, if they are understandable or appropriate, the leader or manager must continue to recognize the team member causing the disturbance as an integral part of the group. Further alienation typically leads only to further disturbance. At these times it would be beneficial for the leader to look at the employee causing the disturbance as being a special employee, one who could use the leader's help or skills, one who remains part of the group, and even one who may be there to teach the leader something. A review of the nature of the communication, power, and corporate climate of the unit would also be beneficial under these circumstances in order to further understand the team member's point of view and avoid further disturbances in the future.

A leader must also have abilities in objective introspection. It is not advisable or even possible to guide or help others unless these skills are developed. It is putting the cart before the horse. A leader recognizing his or her own insecurities will be more easily able to perceive and recognize staff dysfunctions as being symptomatic of systematic dysfunctions. The ego will be more open to rationality once personal problems are more specifically addressed. It takes a secure and mature person to decide that staff is ultimately more important than his or her own ideas are moving forward.

Once new steps are taken after dysfunctions much progress can be made and the company can often be left better off than they were beforehand because of this. The staff can find new means of communication and ways to relate to one another, they can find also find new modes of behavior all together that could even boost their self-esteem or overall well-being. Fortunately for the leader, everyone at the company could then boast of having a manager with a plethora of newfound ideas and attitudes. All these intricacies and regulations tend to make working in a group very complicated at times, but if all of these steps are stuck to and everyone pulls their own weight, the benefits of teamwork can be innumerable.

Conclusion

Thank you for making it through to the end of Dark Psychology. Let's hope this book was as informative and as helpful as possible. We all have a dark side of our psyche whether we admit it or not. Only those who accept and study this dark side can incur the benefits of doing so, and these benefits are some of the greatest we can come across in life, so this book and others like it are some of the greatest resources that we can give ourselves.

Dark psychology could best be described as a study of the human condition in which it becomes normative for people to pray upon others out of criminal and or deviant desires. Often these desires lack specific purpose and are based primarily on basic instinctual desires. Each human has the potential and capacity to victimize other humans, as well as other living creatures, but most of us keep these desires suppressed in order to function successfully in society. Those of us who do not sublimate these dark tendencies are typically representative of the "dark triad": psychopathy, sociopathy, and Machiavellianism, or other mental disorders/psychological disturbances. In this way, dark psychology focuses primarily on the underpinnings (i.e. the thoughts, processing systems, feelings, and behaviors) that are found below the more predatory aspects of our nature, the same ones that go most vigorously against the grain of modern thought concerning human behavior. In this field, we tend to assume that these more abusive, criminal, and deviant behaviors are purposive most of the time, though there are instances in which they seem to have no teleological underpinnings.

Manipulation:

The Most Powerful Techniques to Influencing People, Persuasion, Mind Control, Reading People, NLP. How to Analyze People and Mind Control.

Table of Contents

Introduction..123

Chapter One: Emotional Manipulation..................137

Chapter Two: Covert Manipulation Techniques....148

Chapter Three: NLP Manipulation Techniques......161

Chapter Four: Persuading and Influencing People...170

Chapter Five: Tackling Manipulation in Relationships...191

Chapter Six: Manipulating Mass Opinion as a Public Speaker...199

Chapter Seven: Manipulating With Small-Talk.....205

Conclusion...225

© Copyright 2019 Tony Bennis - All rights reserved.

The following eBook is reproduced below with the goal of providing information that is as accurate and reliable as possible. Regardless, purchasing this eBook can be seen as consent to the fact that both the publisher and the author of this book are in no way experts on the topics discussed within and that any recommendations or suggestions that are made herein are for entertainment purposes only. Professionals should be consulted as needed prior to undertaking any of the action endorsed herein.

This declaration is deemed fair and valid by both the American Bar Association and the Committee of Publishers Association and is legally binding throughout the United States.

Furthermore, the transmission, duplication, or reproduction of any of the following work including specific information will be considered an illegal act irrespective of if it is done electronically or in print. This extends to creating a secondary or tertiary copy of the work or a recorded copy and is only allowed with an expressed written consent from the Publisher. All additional rights reserved.

The information in the following pages is broadly considered to be a truthful and accurate account of facts and as such any inattention, use, or misuse of the information in question by the reader will render any resulting actions solely under their purview. There are no scenarios in which the publisher or the original author of this work can be in any fashion deemed liable for any hardship or damages that may befall them after undertaking information described herein.

Additionally, the information in the following pages is intended only for informational purposes and should thus be thought of as universal. As befitting its nature, it is presented without assurance regarding its prolonged validity or interim quality. Trademarks that are mentioned are done without written consent and can in no way be considered an endorsement from the trademark holder.

Introduction

Ever wondered how some people can always get others to do what they want them to, irrespective of whether the other person wants to do it or not. There is an unspoken almost hypnotic quality that sways people to take the intended action. It can be their words, body language, voice, sneaky strategies or a combination of all. The bottom line- they always have people eating out of their hands and doing what they want them to. While we've all manipulated people in one way or the other in varying degrees throughout our life, some people have mastered the art of manipulating, influencing and persuading people to take the desired action.

While things look all rose-tinted and beautiful on the outside, even with an ideal upbringing, great education and a stellar career, we've all been victims of unsavory tactics used by people to have their way by preying on our feelings, self-worth, and emotions. We've all been part of manipulative relationships where the strings of our feelings and emotions were cleverly controlled by another person to fulfill their needs.

While humans at large thrive on love, kindness, and gratitude, it cannot be denied that it self-centered species. Yes, we are self-serving by nature! While you may not think being selfish or self-serving is a negative trait. Why shouldn't we think about ourselves? However, some folks that this self-centeredness too far. In their bid to serve their needs, they tread upon the feelings and emotions of others.

When people start resorting to intentional, calculated and cunning techniques for having their way is what makes it evil. The intensity of this may vary from person to person depending on their upbringing, environment, personality, experiences, education and several other factors.

We all are guilty of using manipulation at some point, often without realizing it. In the same vein, we are often manipulated by people close to us without realizing that we are being victims of manipulation. And this is precisely what makes it so sinister and insidious. We are made to think, feel and act in a specific way to fulfill another person's need without consideration for our emotions.

For instance, you may be made to feel guilty about working hard or putting in long hours of work even though you are doing it to build a future for your loved ones. Or you'll be made to feel like you are an irresponsible person for taking a break from housework and letting your hair down with friends.

The stark reality about manipulation is that it originates from people who are grappling with issues related to security, self-confidence, and comfort. They attempt to push their luck in a bid to hold other people down for fear of losing them.

Manipulators operate from a deep sense of insecurity. Ironically, what they don't realize is in their bid to hold people down owing to the fear of losing them, they end doing just that. Losing people!

Other times, manipulators are simply out to take advantage of people to serve their cut throat, selfish purposes. They are cold, calculating and ruthless in their acts. There is no regard for the feelings and emotions of their victims. It is a 'dog eat dog' world according to them, and to survive they believe they have to use other people.

Manipulators operate with a point of view that they have to reach their end through whatever means it takes, and if it ends up hurting a few people along the way, so be it. These are people who should actively watch out for and avoid.

The purpose of this book is to make you aware of the sneaky tricks people use for manipulating others. It aims to uncover how people use emotional manipulation, mind control, and persuasion to fulfill their self needs.

When you are able to identify clever manipulative techniques, it becomes easier to guard against them. You'll learn to read warning signs of manipulation and use practical techniques to safeguard your emotions and self-confidence, thus accomplishing complete immunity against people's sly tactics. Manipulation is starkly different from persuasion. While persuasion awards the other person a right to select his/her response to a particular situation, manipulation does give the victim the right to choice. Manipulation has only one way – the way your manipulator wants you to take. There is only a single 'correct choice': the manipulators choice. There is zero regards or concern for your wishes, desires, choices, and emotions. You will pay with hell if you don't pick the choice they want you to.

Typical manipulative tactics include
-Complaining
-Playing victim
-Inducing guilt
-Comparing
-Offering excuses and rationalizing
-Feigning ignorance
-Emotional blackmail
-Evasiveness
-Demonstrating fake concern
-Undermining people
-Blaming others and using "who me?" defenses
-Lying
-Denying
-False flattery
-Intimidation
-Giving the illusion of selflessness
-Shaming
- Using foot in the door techniques
and more

Ever wondered how some people can get others to do exactly what they want? Or how they garner a large following of folks who are more than eager to agree with them or follow their instructions? What are the secret life skills that these people use in the real world to influence people and get them to agree to things?

Mastering the fine art of winning and influencing people is an asset for life. It allows you to bring the best out of others, encourages them to see things from your perspective and ultimately helps them do exactly what you want them to.

It is important to understand that none of the techniques described in the book falls under the dark art strategies of persuading people. Influencing people isn't about destroying their self-esteem to feel great about self.

Au contraire, it is about building them up by encouraging and inspiring them. There are multiple psychological strategies to influence people without making them feel miserable about themselves. We take a hugely positive and constructive approach when it comes to being an amazing influencer and influencing people in the right direction.

Wonder why some influencers inspire a following that goes all out to please them while others can barely get people to acknowledge their instructions? It is about building a connection that drives people in the right direction. Much as pop psychology writers wouldn't want you to believe this, influencing people is more than a bunch of psychological tricks. It runs deeper into people's emotions, their subconscious minds, and their most compelling motivators. According to a legend doing the rounds, Benjamin Franklin had once wanted to please a man who didn't like him much. He went ahead and asked the man to lend him (Franklin) a rare publication. When Franklin received it, he went ahead and thanked the man graciously. The result – the two become great friends.

In Franklin's own words, "He that has once done kindness will be more ready to do you another than he whom you yourself have obliged." Seemingly small acts like (saying a thank you or being gracious) these go a long way in forging bonds where people truly like you and listen to you.

Have you heard of conversation hypnosis? The term has gained much momentum recently and is nothing but a series of techniques used for subconsciously influencing an individual or group's behavior in such as way that they believe their opinion has changed with their own will.

Of course, this area of persuading/ influencing people falls in the grey zone. Influencing people with them believing that it is through their volition can be misleading. It is for every individual to determine whether they want to use these tricks ethically or no. However, there are plenty of proven white-hat techniques to get you started with talking and behaving in a way that makes people sit up and take note.

Effective communication forms the basis of both – your personal and professional encounters. The words, actions, and gestures you use to connect with people help them understand you and make it easier for you to influence their actions in your favor.

Influencing people subtly is all about being a powerful communicator, charismatic influencer and persuasive individual. There are tons of ways through which you can get people to agree with you without being argumentative or negative. This book tells you how. It helps you understand how people react to different stimuli, what drives them to do what they do and how to encourage/inspire them in positive ways. Let's get started right away.

Now that you are fairly competent in identifying emotional and covert manipulation tactics, let's understand what leads people to manipulate others. This may help you deal with them more efficiently.

We've all been victims of everything from pathological lying to being made to feel inadequate to suffering awful smear campaigns. They are beyond reasonable standards of human behavior. What makes people turn into sinister manipulators? What leads manipulators to use the tactics they do? What makes them defy norms of human behavior and turn to underhand techniques to have their way with people? Manipulation is a double edged sword with largely negative connotations. However, in certain circumstances, it can also be used to meet a positive end purpose when no other straight tactic is effective. This handbook of manipulation will not just give you a treasure of manipulation and persuasion tips but also tips for dealing with manipulators in daily life and especially interpersonal relationships. I've taken a comprehensive view of manipulation as a hammer that can be used to destroy things or hit a nail on the wall. Think of it as a powerful tool – you can either use it to build something or destroy it. How you use manipulation is in your hands. While on one hand, you are offered a bunch of manipulation techniques to influence people, on the other, there are tips to safeguard you against sinister or negative manipulation.

Read on to get deeper insights about what makes people manipulate others in ways you'd never imagine.

Why do people manipulate?

Manipulators are constantly living under fear and insecurity. What if this doesn't happen? What if my partner leaves me for someone else? What if someone gains an upper hand over me? They want to win and control all the time to combat an inherent sense of fear.

Where does this fear steam from? It originates from a deep sense of unworthiness. This simply translates as I am certainly not worthy of the good things and people in life, hence these things and people will leave me. To prevent them from leaving me, I must resort to some underhand techniques that will give me absolute control over the people and things I believe I don't deserve. In short, the underlying message is – I am undeserving or unworthy of people and things!

Fear

Why does a person use manipulation to fulfill his/her own agenda? Simple, fear!

It is obvious that manipulators fear that will never be able to gain the desired outcome on their own abilities. That if they act ethically, people and life will not rally reward them positively. They operate from the view that people are life and people are positioned against them. Manipulators fear everyone as their enemy and believe life will not necessarily be favorable to them if they act favorably.

There is a fear that resources are limited and if they don't gain something, others will. They think it's a dog eat dog universe where people have to controlled to help them accomplish the desired result. This control can be in any form – emotional, psychological, financial or practical. They want to control people so they can achieve their desired agenda and out their fear to rest.

Low or No Conscience

Lack of consciousness is another fundamental reason for manipulation. When a person fails to realize that he/she is responsible for their own reality, there is a greater tendency to operate without a conscience. Manipulators don't believe a fair system exists. Also, they've stopped evolving. They don't learn from earlier experiences or try to accomplish a state of congruence between inner emotions and external life.

The view manipulation as a safe or secure world for getting the desired result, despite the fact that these results have not brought them satisfaction in the past. Emotionally and psychologically they keep coming back to square one from time to time, never learning their lesson. To avoid this lesson, they will create another reason to manipulate. Thus, they are caught in a vicious circle of unworthiness or dissatisfaction and then creating another manipulation need.

Manipulation doesn't pay beyond the initial brief fix since the manipulative action is not an authentic, balanced or effective. It is a defense reaction to perceived hurt, unworthiness, fear or insecurity. By being manipulative, the person is attempting to offset these emotions.

Manipulation is a deliberate act that is not aligned with a person's conscience or the greater good. The person doesn't operate with a "we are one" understanding, which means he/she seeks to gain through manipulation by authenticity rather than non-authenticity. Anything gained through non authenticity only leads to narrow victories, ongoing trouble, emptiness or fear, and unworthiness. This creates an even bigger sense of unworthiness. Again unworthiness is a fear of not being worthy of others love and acceptance.

Manipulative folks do not learn, evolve or realize the power of authenticity. Lack of realization of the real power of authenticity and worthiness comes from knowing that one is cherished and accepted for what they really are. In essence, a feeling of unworthiness is often at the core of manipulation.

They Don't Want To Pay The Price Attached to Reach Their Goals

People often manipulate to serve their needs because they do not want to pay the price attached to their goal. They often strive to accomplish the objective or serve their purpose without wanting to give back or pay the price in return.

For instance, if you don't want your partner to leave you, the relationship will take work. You'll have to give your partner love, compassion, understanding, time, loyalty, encouragement, inspiration, a secure future and much more. A manipulator may not want his/her, partner, to leave them but they don't want to pay the price of maintaining a happy, secure and healthy relationship, where the partner will never leave them. They may not want to be loyal or spend much time with their partner, and yet expect them to stay. When people are not ready to pay the price of accomplishing what they want, they may resort to manipulation or underhand techniques to achieve these goals without paying the price attached to them.

Similarly, if a manipulative person wants to be promoted in his/her workplace, rather than working hard, staying past work hours, upgrading their skills or getting a degree, they will simply manipulate their way into the position. The person is not prepared to pay the price or do what it takes to be promoted.

At times, it's deeply ingrained in a person's psyche that wants are bad or that he/she shouldn't have any desires since it makes them come across as selfish. Manipulation then becomes a way to get what they desire or need without even asking for it.

Manipulators realize there is a price attached to everything. A person won't do them a favor without expecting a favor in return. They won't keep getting things if they don't demonstrate kindness and gratitude. A person won't love them or have sex with them without getting commitment, loyalty, and love in return. Manipulators try to push their luck by trying to get something without paying the price attached to it. It is often an easy way out.

They Think They Won't Get Caught

Another reason people manipulate is that they think they can get away with their sneaky acts and that the victims won't realize they are being manipulated. They are also confident that the victim can't do anything even if they manipulation cover is blown.

What gives manipulators the feeling that they won't be caught? Some people come across as inherently clueless, vulnerable, insecure and naïve. These are the type of people manipulators prey on. They believe a person who has low confidence, a low sense of self-worth or is clueless about the ways of the world is less likely to figure out that he/she is being manipulated.

Also, manipulators know that in the event that their manipulation cover is blown, the victim will not be able to do much. They cleverly pick targets who are low on confidence, self-acceptance, body image or sense of self worth. It is easier to play on the vulnerabilities of these people than assertive and self-assure people who won't allow people to take advantage of them.

For example, say a person has low awareness of social dynamics, doesn't understand jokes easily, doesn't identify a prank early, is unable to differentiate between genuine courtesy and sexual advances, can't tell when someone is genuinely attracted to them or simply wants to go to bed with them and other similar social and interpersonal dynamics are likelier to be manipulated.

Manipulators are well aware that their victims can't do anything if they don't even realize that their weaknesses are being misused. They often cash in on the cluelessness of their victims by saying they are imaging things or making something up. An already clueless and unsure person is less likely to question this idea. When you are already reeling under feelings of insecurity, cluelessness, and vulnerability, how difficult is it for the manipulator to take advantage of these feelings by reinforcing them further? Manipulators Manipulators manipulate because they think they can hurt or upset their victims more than the victims can hurt or upset them. They will almost always target people who come across as nice and vulnerable. When people are oblivious to the dishonesty existing within social relationships, they aren't really accustomed to dishonest allegiances. This doesn't equip them with the means to confront or counter dishonesty, which makes them less aware of being manipulated.

They Aren't Able to Accept Their Shortcomings

When people are unable to come to terms with their shortcomings or do not accept the responsibility or accountability for the faults, there is an inherent need to make others feel lesser than them.

If manipulators aren't good enough or feel miserable about themselves, there is a desire to make others feel equally worthless or miserable about themselves. When a person believes he/she is unworthy of someone, they will manipulate the person to feel unworthy too so that they can then gain control over his/her perception that they need the manipulator in their life to feel worthy. By putting others down or gaining control over others, they experience a form of pseudo superiority. If they can't be good enough for others, let's make others feel like they aren't good enough too to retain control over them.

In effect, manipulators don't want their victims to realize that they (the manipulators) aren't good enough or unworthy of them (the victims). The manipulator will therefore carefully cultivate a feeling of helplessness and unworthiness within the victim to keep them hooked to him/her. If a person realizes that he/she is more attractive, intelligent, richer, capable, efficient, self-sufficient, etc., the higher will be their chances of leaving the manipulator. On the other hand, if the manipulator injects a feeling of them not being 'complete', they'll need someone to 'complete' them.

Manipulators are not able to accept their shortcomings or deal with criticism. They are often grappling with deep psychological issues or insecurities. By manipulating others, they do not have to confront their own insecurities to feel higher than others. For someone operating with such a narrow perspective, even a little correction, feedback or criticism can seem like a huge defeat.

People who manipulate don't know how to deal with defeat. When you hesitate to give feedback because the person will get defensive or blow things out of proportion or won't take things in the right spirit, it may be a sign you are dealing with someone who can't come to terms with criticism.

Notice how manipulators will seldom express feelings of gratitude of thankfulness. They find it challenging to be grateful to others because in their view by doing so they are increasing their sense of being obligated to another person, which doesn't give them an upper hand in any relationship.

For example, if you do someone a huge favor, they feel obliged to return that favor which puts you above them in the relationship dynamics until they return the favor.

Manipulators don't want to give you the upper hand by feeling obliged to you. Therefore, they will demonstrate minimal gratefulness so you don't believe you've done something huge for them or that they are obliged to you. The idea is to always be one-up on you and this feel of being indebted to you doesn't make them feel one-up.

Avoiding accepting your shortcomings

When people are unable to come to terms with their shortcomings or do not accept the responsibility or accountability for the faults, there is an inherent need to make others feel lesser than them.

If manipulators aren't good enough or feel miserable about themselves, there is a desire to make others feel equally worthless or miserable about themselves. When a person believes he/she is unworthy of someone, they will manipulate the person to feel unworthy too so that they can then gain control over his/her perception that they need the manipulator in their life to feel worthy. By putting others down or gaining control over others, they experience a form of pseudo superiority. If they can't be good enough for others, let's make others feel like they aren't good enough too to retain control over them.

In effect, manipulators don't want their victims to realize that they (the manipulators) aren't good enough or unworthy of them (the victims). The manipulator will therefore carefully cultivate a feeling of helplessness and unworthiness within the victim to keep them hooked to him/her. If a person realizes that he/she is more attractive, intelligent, richer, capable, efficient, self-sufficient, etc., the higher will be their chances of leaving the manipulator. On the other hand, if the manipulator injects a feeling of them not being 'complete', they'll need someone to 'complete' them.

Manipulators are not able to accept their shortcomings or deal with criticism. They are often grappling with deep psychological issues or insecurities. By manipulating others, they do not have to confront their own insecurities to feel higher than others. For someone operating with such a narrow perspective, even a little correction, feedback or criticism can seem like a huge defeat.

People who manipulate don't know how to deal with defeat. When you hesitate to give feedback because the person will get defensive or blow things out of proportion or won't take things in the right spirit, it may be a sign you are dealing with someone who can't come to terms with criticism.

 Notice how manipulators will seldom express feelings of gratitude of thankfulness. They find it challenging to be grateful to others because in their view by doing so they are increasing their sense of being obligated to another person, which doesn't give them an upper hand in any relationship.

 For example, if you do someone a huge favor, they feel obliged to return that favor which puts you above them in the relationship dynamics until they return the favor. Manipulators don't want to give you the upper hand by feeling obliged to you. Therefore, they will demonstrate minimal gratefulness so you don't believe you've done something huge for them or that they are obliged to you. The idea is to always be one-up on you and this feel of being indebted to you doesn't make them feel one-up.

Chapter One: Emotional Manipulation

While everyone is guilty of using manipulation (knowingly or unknowingly) at some point, what makes emotional manipulators different is they habitually trample upon people's emotions and feelings to serve their own selfish needs. It is a way of life for some people to use other people's feelings in a bid to increase their psychological hold or superiority over the person.

1. Play on people's fears. Emotional manipulators tend to blow facts out of proportion and highlight only specific points in a bid to instill fear in you. For example, a man who doesn't want his wife to pursue a full-time career outside the house may tell her something like "research reveals 60 percent of all divorces happen when both partners are engaged in full-time careers", sneakily hiding the fact that there can be reasons other than the woman's career or job. This is cleverly constructed to prey on the woman's fear of losing the relationship is she gives in to her ambitions.

2. The actions and words shouldn't match. Emotional manipulators tell you exactly what they think you want to hear but will rarely follow it up with action. They will pledge commitment and support. However, when it comes to act upon their commitment they will make you feel guilty for coming up with unreasonable demands.

At one point they'll tell you how fortunate they are to know a person like you, and the next they'll be slamming you for being a burden. This is a clever tactic for undermining a person's belief about their sanity. Emotional manipulators will keep saying things that suit their purpose and suddenly mold a perception to the contrary by doing the opposite of what they said to misbalance sanity.

This also comes at a price, which they'll sneakily claim in future. As an emotional manipulator, you are constantly reminding people about how you helped them and use that as leverage to make them feel obliged to you. If you perpetually remind them of a favor you willingly did for them, which makes the other person feel they owe you something, there are high chances you are being emotionally manipulated.

3. Become masters at distributing guilt. Few people leverage the power of guilt like practiced manipulators. Emotional manipulators induce guilt in other people to serve their needs. If someone brings up an issue that's been bothering them for discussion, manipulators make them feel guilty about feeling the way they do, however, justified these feelings may seem. Emotional manipulators make people feel guilty for mentioning the issue. When someone doesn't mention the issue, make you feel miserable for not being open and talking about it.

Keep stewing guilt in you, irrespective of the direction of the other person's thoughts and actions. One way or another, find reasons to make you feel guilty. Anything they choose to do is wrong. Irrespective of the problems the other person may be having collectively, an emotional manipulator will always make them feel it is only your fault. Manipulators blame people for everything unfortunate happening in their life and build a strong sense of guilt within them. If you want to get people to do what you want them to, induce a sense of guilt and regret. Guilt is one of the strongest manipulation forces that drive people to delve deep and give in to what you want them to.

Emotional manipulators prey on their victims by posing themselves to be the victims. They lead their victims into believing that it is always their fault irrespective of whether they are truly responsible or not. The blame is always assigned to the victim with the manipulator playing the victim. This is done in effect to move responsibility from the manipulator's shortcomings to blaming the victim, which is done with the intention of inducing guilt in them. When a victim feels a sense of guilt of self-blame for the unpleasant situation, it becomes simpler for the manipulator to get them to take the desired action.

Manipulators concentrate on how the other person got them to do something or how it is the other person's fault for which they (the manipulators) are suffering. It is always the other person who is making the manipulator angry, hurt and upset. As a manipulator, you seldom accept accountability or responsibility for your own actions.

Let us consider an example here to illustrate this emotional manipulation strategy even more effectively. Your partner is upset with you for forgetting your anniversary. The reasonable thing to do in such a scenario would be to apologize for the goof up and make it up to them later by giving them a surprise or a nice gift. However, manipulators resort to playing blame games. The blame is turned on its head in the direction of the other person. You make the other person feel guilty about making you feel so terrible about forgetting an anniversary. There is a tendency to introduce a sense of guilt so the other person can do what you want them to.

So to justify forgetting your anniversary to your partner and inducing a sense of guilt, you may speak about how stressed, tired, busy and exhausted you have been, and how inconsiderate it is on their part to blame you for forgetting an anniversary when you've been working really hard on a project lately. We have in effect made the other person feel guilty for a reasonable expectation. The tables are being turned on them to avoid taking on the blame of forgetting the anniversary.

Hardcore manipulators will not stop there, however, and instead they will go one step further, and go over all the instances when the other person has forgotten important occasions in a bid to justify their own forgetfulness. You make the other person feel like it is indeed their fault for expecting you to remember all dates when you are stressed with work. It acts as a sort of justification for your forgetfulness. Master manipulators know how to weave a sense of guilt within the other person's consciousness to lead them into taking the intended action. They use blame and guilt generously to fulfill their needs.

For instance, let us assume an individual brings up something that is working on their mind for a long time now. Manipulators will most probably make them feel like they are making a mountain out of a molehill, and that it isn't a big deal. You make the other person feel guilty about making an issue out of a seemingly non-issue. Rather than accepting their troubles and committing to work on them, the tables are turned on the other person to make them feel guilty for mentioning the issue or their true feelings. This manipulation technique is primarily used in personal relationships when one person opens up to the other partner, and the latter turns back and blames him/her for bringing up something so trivial. You make the other person feel guilty about everything they do. If they remain silent, you may accuse them of not sharing their feelings or not trusting you with a resolution for their problems. If they happen to share their feelings, you blame them for making issues where there are none. There is constant guilt stirring to make the other person feel that they are always at fault to meet your own agenda.

All the other person's actions are attributed to him/her or presented/positioned as their fault until they meet your agenda. At the same time, you don the role of the unfortunate victim. Inducing a sense of guilt is, in fact, one of the most powerful manipulation strategies for getting someone to obey you. This becomes even more effective on folks who suffer from low self-esteem or reduced self-confidence levels.

For example, if you want to get someone to take the desired action, confidently rattle off a list of favors you've done for them or all the instances when you have gone out of the way to help them. Later, follow this by how you've felt let down every time you've expected something from them. You turn into a projected victim who did all the wonderful things to help them out in their time of need, and they turn into the ungrateful beings that do not stand up to your needs when required. This is subtly playing on the victims' minds to make them think like they are not returning the favor or being thankless. Manipulators often get the other person to do what they want by saying something like, "It is fine Roger, I cannot expect anything more from you. It is really my fault that I keep expecting a lot from you and our relationship. This induces a sense of guilt in the other person as if he/she is letting the manipulator down, which may or may not be the case. You are telling them they are always disappointing you and that you can't expect anything more from them.

Ever observed how we play manipulation games and introduce a sense of guilt within our personal relationships a lot of times? Note how the elderly make their children experience a sense of guilt by mentioning how the latter never have enough time for them.

When teens ask for permission from their parents about overnight outings and late party deadlines and are refused, they will go on about how the parents are not letting them live their life or are coming across as too suffocating, overprotective and overbearing. They will talk about how they need to negotiate the world around them sooner or later without their parents being around to protect them all the time.

We all know that one person who is forever blaming other people or circumstances for their shortcomings. They will strategically utilize their sense of helplessness to get the other person to take the desired action. Manipulators give others the impression that they (the other person) have decided their (the manipulator's) fate through their actions and choices, often negatively. Then they will make the victim feel like they are responsible for the manipulator's woes now, and they should make good the damage.

The victims begin accepting this notion that they are responsible for a negative situation created for the manipulator and often respond in the affirmative to the manipulator's request to make it up to the seemingly negative thing they've been led to believe they have done. The manipulator positions himself/herself as someone who needs help and doomed if they don't receive timely help. The other person feels terrible and ends up doing as you want them to because to some extent they feel responsible for your helplessness or unfortunate situation.

4. Play the victim. Where emotional manipulation is concerned, nothing that happens is ever your mistake. Irrespective of your actions, you always blame someone else for their failings.

You harp on how they were made you do something. If they get angry or hurt, you are the one responsible for building unreasonable expectations. If they get angry or upset, you are responsible for hurting them. There is zero accountability for any action.

For example, if a person forgets their partner's birthday, and the partner gets upset about it, they'll generally apologize and promise to make good for it in the future. However, an emotionally manipulative person will not just deny it is their fault; they will also make their partner feel miserable for blaming them.

They will take off about how stressed they've been off late owing to something the partner has done that it's just impossible for them to remember it. The manipulator will go a step ahead and remind you of instances where you've forgotten something important to justify their fault.

5. Emotional manipulators expect too much, way too soon. From an interpersonal relationship to a business association, emotional manipulators are always taking the highway, while overlooking a few steps along the way. They may share too much too early in a relationship and expect the other person to do the same.

Their vulnerability, transparency, and sensitivity are a clever ruse. This is a 'special' charade to make you feel a part of their inner circle. Slowly and insidiously, you'll not just feel sorry about their feelings but also responsible for it.

6. Emotional manipulators belittle your faith in understanding reality. These people, you must hand it to them, are exceptionally skilled liars and cheats. They will confidently insist something happened when it didn't and deny it happened when it did. They do in such a devious and underhanded manner that you begin questioning your own sanity.

For example, if you suspect your partner of having and confront them about it, the emotionally manipulative partner with outright deny it (even though it is the truth), and in turn make you feel like an insane, suspicious person who doesn't have a grip over reality.

Even though your suspicion is not unfounded, you'll be made to feel guilty about spying around and not trusting your partner. It'll come to a point where you will begin questioning your own suspicious nature and sanity. I am sure many of you are nodding your head in agreement to this!

I know by now you've already identified such people and relationships and chances are weren't even aware of these snarky, insidious tactics when we were being manipulated.

7. Everyone must feel the way they do. Wow, this is another sneaky emotional manipulation technique used to suck other people into their emotional state. The emotional manipulator

wants everyone to feel like they are feeling. If they are in a foul mood, everyone around should be aware of it.

However, it doesn't end there. Not only should everyone know how they are feeling, but they should also be sucked into the emotional state of the manipulator. Whatever other people are feeling or experiencing should be dropped down and they should instantly match the emotional frequency of the manipulator. This makes people around them feel like they are responsible for the emotional manipulator's feelings, and they alone should fix it.

8. Eagerness to help becomes a burden later. Emotional manipulators will volunteer to help initially (and pretty eagerly at that) only to make themselves look like martyrs later. They will act like what they initially agreed to do is a huge burden.

If you remind them that they committed to the task, they'll turn around and make you feel like a paranoid person despite them appearing eager to help. The objective? To induce a feeling of guilt, feeling obliged towards them and probably even questioning your sanity!

9. One-upmanship games. Irrespective of the intensity of your problems and challenges, they will always make it come across as their problems are much worse. They will attempt to undermine the authenticity of your problems by constantly reinforcing how bigger their problems or challenges.

They'll make you feel guilt for complaining about 'trivial' things when they are facing serious issues. The goal? You don't have any reason to complain about your 'non-serious', while they have every right to keep reminding you of their 'serious' problems. In other words, they want you to shut up and stop complaining about your problems, and always be one-up in every situation.

10. They know your emotional buttons and how to press them at will. We all have our emotional weak spots. Emotional

manipulators are cleverly aware of your weak spots and do not hesitate to use them for serving their own sinister objectives. They will use knowledge of your weak spots against you.

For example, if you are insecure about your appearance, they will pass snide remarks about everything from your clothes to your weight. Again, if you are worried about an upcoming speech, they will prey on your fears by telling you how tough, picky and judgmental the audience is. They use awareness of your emotions not to make you feel better but to manipulate you into feeling worse.

11. Emotional manipulators use humor to take a dig at your perceived weaknesses to disempower you or make you feel inadequate. Notice how some people are perpetually making critical or snide remarks about their partner or friend, often in the garb of humor. The idea is to make the other person feel inadequate, inferior or insecure.

Emotional manipulators attempt to disempower the person by playing on his/her perceived weaknesses. The remarks encompass everything from the person's appearance to their old phone to their skills. They make sarcastic and seemingly funny comments about everything, including the fact that you walked in 30 seconds late.

The idea is to make you look bad and feel worse about yourself. This way the manipulator tries to gain psychological dominance over you, unfortunately without you even realizing it (now you do, right?). Undermining you makes you perceive yourself as inferior, which automatically gives them the much needed psychological superiority.

12. Emotional manipulators constantly judge and criticize you to make you feel inferior. In the above example, we saw how manipulators use covert techniques to disempower you by disguising their snide remarks as humor. However, here the emotional manipulator outright dismisses, marginalizes,

criticizes and ridicules you in a bid to main psychological superiority over you.

Their premise is if they make you feel inadequate and off-balance, their chances of getting you to do whatever they want to increase. You will stop believing in your abilities, sanity, and worth, which will help them wield greater control over your thoughts, emotions and actions.

The emotional aggressor will intentionally foster the feeling that something is not right with you, and that however hard you try, you won't be good enough. Significantly, the emotional manipulator will emphasize the weaknesses without offering constructive or positive solutions or assisting you in meaningful ways to overcome the negatives.

13. Emotional manipulators will give you the silent treatment. Another art emotional manipulators have mastered is the art of giving people the silent treatment to pressurize them into doing what the manipulator wants. They will intentionally make you wait and sow seeds of doubt, insecurity, and uncertainty in your mind. Emotional manipulators use silence as leverage to get you to do what they want by keeping you emotionally deprived or insecure.

Being at the receiving end of the silent treatment is a warning sign you are dealing with an emotional manipulator. It is a type of emotional abuse through which contempt is demonstrated through nonverbal acts such as remaining silent or withdrawing all communication.

The silent treatment is used as a tool to incite their victims into doing something specific or make them feel inadequate by the refusal to acknowledge their presence. If your actions don't match what the manipulator wants you to do, they will utilize the silent treatment for communicating their disappointment and punishing their victims.

14. Pretend play. Yes, they can play dumb too whenever needed. They will pretend that they don't understand what

exactly you want or what you desire from them. This is one of the sneaky passive-aggressive tricks, where should be their responsibility, becomes yours. So the onus of what is essentially their responsibility is thrown on your shoulders. This is often used by people who are trying to hide something or avoid an obligation.

15. Raising voice and demonstrating negative emotions. Some emotional manipulators know how to use the power of their voice and body language to coerce you into their demands. They will often raise their voice as a type of aggressive manipulation with the belief that if they sound intimidating enough with their voice, tone and body language, you will invariably submit to their demands. The aggressor-like voice is often combined with intimating body language such as exaggerated gestures and standing to increase the effect of their aggressive manipulative actions.

16. Negative surprises as a norm. Whoa! Don't these people know how to throw you off balance with their negative surprises in an obvious attempt to gain a psychological advantage over you? They will suddenly come up with some information about not being able to do something or deliver a commitment as promised.

Typically, the negative information is thrown on you without any forewarning to catch you off guard. You are left with no time to come up with a counter move. Emotional manipulators are wolves in sheep's clothing and won't spare a single opportunity to cause discomfort, hurt or harm to you if you get in the way.

Chapter Two: Covert Manipulation Techniques

Recognizing covert manipulation tactics is tricky because unlike overt manipulation these aren't obvious or in your face. They are often underhanded techniques of trying to gain control of the victim's thoughts, feelings, and decisions. It is aimed at bringing down a person's sense of self-worth and destroying their belief in their perceptions. When you learn the manipulator's game, you can play it better than them. Manipulation undermines the victim's ability to make conscious decisions and act in accordance with their interests. Instead, they become mere puppets in someone else's hands. Manipulators don't value people's personal values, desires, and boundaries. In plain words, they'll make you do something you wouldn't normally do.

So what are the most widely used covert manipulation tactics and how do you spot it in your everyday life? Read on to de-bluff people's covert manipulation games. While these can be used as manipulation strategies by you to get people to do what you want them to, ensure that you do not overuse them or try to lend them as much of a positive twist as possible.

1. Create a false sense of intimacy. Notice how people are constantly sharing intimate information about themselves in the early stages of a relationship? They will talk about their family, backgrounds, and lives (often portraying themselves as victims as circumstances) in a bid to win your sympathy, while also creating an illusion of intimacy.

2. Introduce other people in the picture in a bid to make you insecure. Again, some people are always trying to create a sense of insecurity or discomfort in their victims by introducing other people into the picture. For example, your partner may talk about meeting an ex-girlfriend/boyfriend or good friend to make you feel insecure.

Of course, not everyone who meets friends or ex-partners is being manipulative. However, covert manipulators are constantly using this tactic of introducing other people into the picture to unsettle their partner. When a person is trying to pit other people against you to make you feel inadequate, you can be sure it's a covert manipulation tactic.

3. Another covert manipulation technique is 'foot in the door', which is fairly easy to recognize. It involves making a small request that the victim agrees to, which is subsequently followed by the actually intended request. It is tougher to refuse once the victim says agrees to the initial request.

Foot in the door technique as the name suggests, the objective here is to get your foot in the door until you are comfortably positioned or placed to ask for what you want the other person to do. It can be traced back to the time when door to door salespeople placed their foot in door to prevent prospective buyers from slamming the door on their face. Placing their foot in the door offered them more time to keep the conversation going, and ultimately make a sale. This ingenious manipulation strategy is effectively used across settings even today.

How can the foot in the door manipulation strategy be effectively used in today's scenario?

It is just as simple and efficient, only now you are making headway into a person's mind instead of their door. Start by building a rapport with the person. Attempt to break the ice by making a small request. Remember, the key is to make a small request, which is the other person can easily fulfill. What you are actually doing is slipping your foot in the door to develop a rapport with the person to get them to concede to a bigger or the actual demand later. If you straight away ask for what you actually intend to get them to do for you, they may refuse. Begin with a request that isn't too challenging to meet for the other person. Go for the kill gradually and steadily. Move to the actual request slowly and subtly.

You are trying to get the person to say a series of 'yes' in a sequence before moving in to the actual kill. This will psychologically reduce the chances of the person breaking the pattern and saying no for the final or actual request. This is precisely why psychologists and behavioral experts urge salespersons to ask their prospects several questions that result in a 'yes'. According to research in the field of psychology and behavioral science, if a prospect answers in the affirmative to six questions in a sequence, there are higher chances of them purchasing your product/service or taking the desired action.

Use this information to your advantage by asking people six questions in a series, where they are likelier to reply in the affirmative. The strategy works at a subconscious level and is worth trying.

We launch a sequence of positive replies that make it almost impossible for the other person's subconscious mind to refuse our final request. Once a person starts a loop of responding to your requests in a positive manner, subconsciously it becomes tough to break the pattern, and suddenly offer a negative response.

This is exactly what salespersons in the earlier times did. They placed their foot in the door and offered themselves extra 3-4 minutes with prospects to build the sales pitch momentum, develop rapport and make a sale. Now let's think about the same strategy in today's setting. How do you give yourself that tiny opening that you can eventually cash upon by getting people to do what you desire?

Let us take an example to understand how this manipulation or persuasion can be applied in today's scenario. Jane is finishing the project that requires her to build a model of the nine planets. She asks her mom to help out by creating a rough model for the nine planets project. Of course, her mother does the rough sketch, collects all the required materials to build the model, and keeps everything ready for Jane to make her project. Jane then goes on to request her mom to put all the various pieces together. She does as requested. Finally, Jane's mom finishes doing the entire assignment with no inputs or effort from Jane. Jane used the foot in the door strategy to manipulate her mother into completing her project for her instead of directly asking her to do in the beginning. If Jane would've directly requested her mother to complete the project, she would've refused point blank. However, she got her mom to say a series of 'yes' with small requests that eventually ended with her mother completing the entire project.

This manipulation and persuasion technique for first studied by Fraser and Freeman during the 20th century! The goal is to get people to respond or agree to a tiny and simple request leading to a bigger 'yes.' The psychologist duo realized that once people agree to a seemingly tiny request, the chances of them responding in an affirmative to bigger requests increase. In this example, Jane got her mom to finish the entire assignment by placing together several pieces of the task and getting her to agree to each of these smaller tasks or requests. Once the initial tiny request of creating a rough sketch for the model was agreed upon, Jane could manage to get her mother to meet her larger request. This wouldn't have been the case had she requested her mother to complete the entire project at the outset.

While utilizing the foot in the door strategy, make sure the request is tiny enough for people to not reply in the negative. At the same time, it should be sufficiently important to give the other person the feeling that they have done a good deed by responding to your request in a positive manner. Keep the request positive so other people do not think isn't worth their while to fulfill it. Ensure the request is something that a person will be willing to do without many external influences like rewards or pressure.

If someone refuses the actual request, they'll come across as someone who agrees to something they don't intend to do. When they object to the real request, you will quickly turn the tables to come across as the aggrieved party. It stops being about your demands since you are now the injured ones. The focus shifts to your complaints and they are placed on the defensive now. Sometimes, warnings and worry about their well being is cleverly hidden as a concern. Manipulators are forever trying to undermine the other person's choices and decisions in an attempt to shake their self-confidence or sense of self-worth. Again, this manipulation technique must be used with sufficient caution and care.

4. "Snakes in Suits" – In their publication *Snakes in Suits*, Robert Hare and Paul Babaik advise how people should guard against manipulators who offer out of place and excessive compliments. It is a huge manipulation red flag. Focus keenly on what's next. Keep questioning yourself, what exactly does this person want from me?

5. Force Teaming. Have you noticed how some people are always creating a forced sense of team spirit or shared purpose where none exists? Typical phrases used by them include, we're one team", "how do we handle this as a team", "we've done it now" etc. They purportedly try to portray that you both are involved in something as a team.

In such a situation, how can you tell if the person is being genuinely helpful or simply trying to manipulate you? Do feel a strange sense of discomfort while accepting their help? Are their words congruent with their body language? (more on body language later) Is the person giving you an option to refuse help? Are they taking your refusal in the right spirit? If no, you may be dealing with a covert manipulator, who is trying to manipulate you under the guise of offering you help.

6. Flattering First Impression. Practiced manipulators often make a stellar first impression. They use a bunch of enticing characteristics such as flawless manners, attractive looks, charismatic smile and courtesy to throw their victims off guard about their real intentions. Yes, they exist beyond the movies, where con men and women are shown to be these stereotypical characters with a dazzling personality and a glib tongue.

With manipulators, what appears on the surface is not the truth. However, with time and observation, you will notice the cracks in their cleverly worn masks. When it gets really sadistic, the silence is used to torture their victims. For instance, a co-worker talks to everyone at work but ignores you or refuses to have any conversation with you.

7. Covert manipulators will appear to be selfless by keeping their real intentions, ambitions, goals, and agendas cleverly cloaked. Their true intentions are hidden under the garb of a selfless cause. This one's tricky to indentify. These are the people who will act like they are working hard on behalf of another person while hiding their true ambition for power and dominance over others.

 For example, a covert manipulator will give his/her manager the impression that they are willing to put in extra hours of work when the manager is away on vacation only to fulfill their ambition of eventually taking over the manager's position.

8. Gas lighting. The term gas lighting as a covert manipulation technique comes from the play of the same name which was later adapted into films. It has also been used in literature and psychological research.

Using the gas lighting technique, a manipulator will twist reality to fulfill their objectives. Irrespective of the truth, they have tricks up their sleeves for making you think that it is indeed your fault for not being able to perceive things correctly. It is so deeply ingrained into your mind that you stop trusting your perceptions and instead accept the manipulator's contrived version of the truth. The technique is intended to make you feel so mentally incompetent that you stop trusting your version of reality. It gets to a point where if someone tries to challenge your perceptions, you are mistrustful of them.

9. Rationalization. Rationalization is a technique through which a manipulator offers some form of justification for a hurtful, offensive or inappropriate action. What makes the technique so tough to spot is that the explanation given often enough sense for any reasonable individual to buy it. Rationalization fulfills three fundamental purposes including, eliminating resistance manipulators may have about their inappropriate action, keeping others from pointing fingers at them and helping the manipulator justify his/her actions in the victim's eyes.

Manipulators who use rationalization will typically behave very affectionately at times and then suddenly act distant or cold. When the victim gets tired of their behavior and confronts them or avoids them, they will most likely scream or cry and mention how they have been depressed or upset off late and how you are such a bad person for confronting them about their seemingly inappropriate behavior when you are one who is behaving insensitively.

They will move you to tears with how stressful their life is, even apologize for it at times. However, within the next few days, they'll repeat the pattern. Manipulators are remarkable performers. They can play the victim's role with ease. They can fake emotions, cry at will, laugh when they want to and pretend to be sad or happy on demand. Carefully examine the acts of people who 'love you' or forever try to gain sympathy.

10. Nitpicking and goal post moving. The difference between positive criticism and negative/destructive criticism is a manipulator will come up with near impractical standards and personal attacks. These self-proclaimed critics pretend to help your development, when in fact, they don't want to see you improve. They are simply operating with the intention of nitpicking on you, pulling you down and making you a scapegoat in every possible manner.

Covert manipulators are masters in the art of 'moving goalposts' to ensure they are never short of reasons to be disappointed with you. Even when you present evidence to validate your stand or act to fulfill their request, they will come up with another lofty expectation for you to meet or ask for more proof to validate your argument. Yes, who said dealing with manipulators was easy?

For example, they may start by picking on you for not having a successful career. When you have a successful career, they'll question you for not being a multi-millionaire yet. When that expectation is met, they'll demand why your personal-work life is never balanced. The goal posts will keep changing and the expectations will rise higher in a bid to make you feel incompetent in some way or the other.

One of the easiest ways to spot a manipulator is to observe if they are constantly instilling a sense of unworthiness in you or forever making you feel whatever you do is never good enough. A genuine or constructive will never induce a sense of unworthiness in you. They will gently point your limitations and often suggest ways to overcome it. Manipulators, on the other hand, will never offer suggestions to help you overcome your limitations.

If a person is constantly criticizing you without helping you overcome the issue or limitations in a meaningful way, you may most likely be a victim of covert manipulation. They will cleverly present it as constructive criticism even if it just nitpicking without offering solutions.

If a person keeps demanding more proof for validating your argument or keeps raising their expectations, their aim is obviously not to understand you better. They are attempting to provoke you into experiencing a sense of inadequacy or that you have to keep proving yourself all the time.

11. Withholding apology. Covert manipulators will seldom apologize for their actions. Instead, they will deny, lie or shift the blame to avoid accepting responsibility for their act. Be mindful of this covert manipulation technique by examining if the person apologizes and accepts responsibility for their mistakes.

If a person constantly makes you feel like you are blowing things out of proportion or over reacting rather than apologizing, you are most probably dealing with a covert manipulator. Manipulators have a strong urge to be right even at the cost of mending a relationship. Withholding apology is just another controlling mechanism for them.

12. Undermining your success. I once had a friend who was constantly made to feel guilty about being successful by his partner. He was creating a promising future for them and their future kids, but she constantly made him feel terrible about the fact that he worked so hard and barely had time for her. She accused him of being selfish and thinking only about his goals when it fact, he was building a future for their family. When you tell your partner or a close friend about a promotion or a new job offer how should they usually react? They should be delighted you are progressing in life. Those who truly care about you will want to see you succeed. Manipulators will constantly try to underplay and undermine your success. They will always find some way to instill negativity in any form related to your success story. This

arises from a clear sense of insecurity that you are now becoming more self-sufficient, and will no longer need them. The feeling that the more successful you become, the less they'll be able to control you leads them to behave in an irrational manner. Thus, they'll make you feel miserable about your success. Sometimes, they'll even get angry for no apparent reason. One of their biggest concerns is that financial independence will give you the ability to survive without their help. This prospect can be threatening for a person who is accustomed to having his/her friend or partner depend on him/her excessively.

13. Fear-Relief Cycle or using fear followed by relief. This is yet another covert manipulation strategy that is utilized in a variety of settings, popularly used by advertisers, brand managers, and marketers to persuade their target consumer group into taking the desired action in favor of their products or services. How does the fear and relief chain work? It essentially acts on a psychological level that makes the entire process effective.

This covert manipulation technique comprises playing on the other person's fears to get them to take the required action in your favor. You introduce a sense of fear and get them to think of the worst that can happen in a particular situation. This is quickly followed up by offering a sense of relief. The person will experience a huge sense of relief and positivity that helps them make a fast decision to meet your agenda.

Let us look at an example. You begin by saying something like, "When I wore your earrings at the party the other night, I heard a snapping sound. I was sure the earring broke. Later, I realized that my sister was actually watching a video on her tablet. Isn't that funny? That reminds me, can I borrow those beautiful earrings again for an upcoming event?

What did you just do? You took the person through a curve of fear followed by relief to bring about a quick change in their emotions at the psychological level to help them take action in the desired direction. The other person feels a huge sense of relief that nothing actually happened to their earrings and they are in a proper condition. They slip into a more receptive, flexible and positive state of mind, which makes it simpler for you to get him/her to do what you desire.

Start by sowing seeds of insecurity and fear in the other person. Make them imagine the worst that can happen within the given situation. Then, tactfully follow this up by providing a solution or diving into a narrative about how things were not as bad as the other person thought or imagined. Once the person realizes that things are indeed not as unfortunate as they had imagined, it will become easier to get them in a more receptive and agreeable frame of mind. The quick whirlwind of roller coaster like emotions makes it easier for the other person to get into a more positive frame of mind once some hope is offered to combat their fear. This positivity can be used to get them to do what you want them to.

Think about how it impacts the person at a psychological level. The victim goes through a cycle or pattern of powerful emotions. Fear is a huge emotion that is capable of getting people to take a lot of quick actions. However, it should be used sparingly. Beyond a point, if people realize that you simply use fear as a tool to manipulate them, they will stop responding to it. Fear makes people uncomfortable and nervous. This is then immediately followed by positivity, a huge sense of relief and instant hope.

Let us look at another example to understand how a consumerist driven market use this manipulation strategy to the hilt when it comes to getting people to make purchase related decisions. Almost every insurance salesperson uses the fear-relief cycle on his/her prospects to get them to buy insurance from him/her. They will introduce a sense of fear, stress panic and anxiety to the inform prospects about how their valuables are always at a risk of getting lost or destroyed under several unfortunate circumstances. They will talk about thefts, fire, robbery and other unfortunate situations where your precious things can get lost, destroyed or stolen. This will be followed up by bringing in a solution – buy an insurance policy so you don't suffer any financial losses. This fear-relief cycle technique brings in some measure of hopefulness, surety, security, and relief within a person to lead them into making a fast buying decision. They think of the policy as the solution or ray of hope when it comes to protecting the worth of their valuables.

14. Ask Big and Scale Back. This is the opposite of the foot in the door technique. In psychological jargon, this is also referred to as the "door in the face" technique. It starts off by making a ridiculously unreasonable request from someone (which they are guaranteed to reject). Later, you return and ask for something much more feasible and less ridiculous (what you were after in the first place).

It may sound insane, but the idea is to make the other person feel sorry about refusing your initial request (even though it was obviously ridiculous). The next time you come up with something more reasonable, the person will feel obliged to comply. This is like the payback for refusing your earlier request, and they feel more bound to help you than another person. Several companies and salespeople use this technique to sell to their customers.

15 Fake confidence. Alright, so you dress up attractively, sport a sharply groomed appearance, carry the most stylish accessories, and still wonder why people don't listen to you, follow you or subscribe o your views.

Chances are, you are missing the most vital accessory – confidence. Yes, you have to slay the demon of low confidence if you really want to inspire the faith of others. The clothes, accessories, and grooming can only carry you up to a point.

One of the most fundamental principles of confidence is that you can totally fake it even when you don't feel it. It is all about your body language, voice, expressions, and gestures (which are fortunately in your control). You can pretend to be a highly confident persona even when you're feeling like a lemon from within.

Our body language invariably impacts our mental state and vice versa. When you act confident for a long time, you end up confusing the brain into believing that you are indeed a very confident person. The brain then automatically reprograms itself and directs the body to be confident, thinking it goofed up somewhere. So, what starts off as a pretentious act actually leads to you transforming into a more confident and self-assured individual.

You have to act all self-assured and confident if you truly want the other person to buy what you are saying. If you don't look convinced about something, there's a slim chance you are going to be able to convince other people about it. Therefore confidence is one of the most vital accessories for a manipulator.

Chapter Three: NLP Manipulation Techniques
What is Neuro Linguistic Programming?

Neuro Linguistic Programming or NLP in simplest terms is the programming language of your mind. We've all had instances where we attempted to communicate with someone who doesn't speak our language. The outcome? They didn't understand us!

You go to a restaurant aboard and ask for a fancy steak but end up receiving insipid stew owing to the misinterpretation of language and codes.

This is precisely what happens when we try to communicate with our subconscious mind. We think we are commanding it to give us happier relationships, more money, a better job, and other similar things. However, if that's not what is actually showing up, something is being lost in translation. The subconscious/unconscious mind has the power to help us accomplish our goals only if we program it using codes it recognizes and understands.

If you are asking your unconscious mind for steak and receiving stew, it is time to speak its language. Think of NLP as a user manual for the brain. When people master NLP, they become fluent in the language of the subconscious mind, which is excellent when it comes to re-programming their and other people's thoughts, ideas, and beliefs. This gives them the power to influence and persuade people, and on the downside even manipulate them.

Neuro Linguistic Programming is a set of techniques, methods, and tools for enhancing communication with deeper layers of our brain. It is an approach that combines personal development, psychotherapy, and communication. Its creators (John Grinder and Richard Bandler) claim that there is a strong link between language, behavior patterns and neurological processes, which can be used for enhancing learning and personal development.

Influence versus Manipulation
So, do you believe a hammer is a tool of utility or destruction? Well, depends on how you use it right? Or what purpose you use it for?

NLP is potent when it comes to getting people to do what you want them to. It is the hammer that can be used to fix a nail in the wall or destroy a piece of wood. Similarly, NLP can be used to build something positive or it can be used for a destructive purpose (manipulation).

NLP and Manipulation have nearly the same meaning. Both are about generating the desired effect on other people without obvious exertion. However, one key difference between influence and manipulation is that the latter is meant to influence others to meet the manipulator's selfish goals through means that can be unfair, unlawful, sneaky, or insidious. Things are contrived through underhand methods to turn out in favor of the manipulator. A manipulator often preys on the insecurities, fears, and guilt of other people. In turn, victims of manipulation feed dissatisfied, frustrated, trapped and unhappy.

Conversely, influence is the ability to inspire people in an admirable, charismatic and honorable way. We are often inspired by influential people and aspire to model our life on theirs. There is a general feeling of positivity related to them, and we feel positively impacted in their company. Not every influence is positive, which is why we do use terms such as "bad influence" to signify a person's negative effect on us. However, manipulation is never categorized as good or bad. It always operates with sinister motives. That is the primary difference between influence and manipulation.

Influence is a double edged sword that can be used positively and negatively, while manipulation only operates with a negative, narrow and selfish perspective to meet the objectives of the manipulator.

While manipulation has self-centered and questionable motives, influence can also be positive. In contrast to manipulation, influence has positive connotations, which considers other people's needs, goals and desires. Don't we as parents want to influence our children to lead happier and healthier lives? Similarly, as a manager, we want to influence our team to put in their best efforts.

Just like the hammer discussed above, people can use NLP for positively or negatively influencing people to meet their own selfish objectives (manipulation). NLP is a mind control tool that can do both – build and damage. The techniques mentioned here can be used to spot NLPers manipulating you or for you to manipulate other people. Again – you have a powerful tool in your possession that can either be used constructively or destructively.

How is NLP Used For Manipulating People?

NLP training is conducted in a pyramid-like structure, with sophisticated techniques reserved for high-end seminars. It is a complex subject (whoever said anything related to the human mind would ever be easy). However, to simplify a complicated concept, NLPers or people who practice NLP pay keen attention to people they work with. They watch everything from eye movements to skin flushes to pupil dilation to determine what type of information people are processing.

Through observation, NLPers can tell which side of the brain is dominant in a person. Similarly, they can tell what sense is the most active within the person's brain. The eye movements can determine how their brain stores and uses information. It is also easy to decipher whether the person is stating facts (telling the truth) or making up facts (lying) by looking at his/her eye movements.

After gathering this invaluable information, NLP manipulator will subtly mirror and mimic their victims (including speech, body language, mannerisms, verbal linguistic patterns and more) to give a feeling of being "one among them."

NLPers will fake social clues to lead their victims into dropping their guard and entering a more open, receptive and suggestible state of mind, where they become ready to absorb whatever information their mind is fed with. Manipulators will cleverly use language that focuses on a person's predominant senses.

For example, if a person is focused on his/her visual sense, the NLP manipulator will most likely use it to his/her advantage optimally by saying something like, "Do you see where I am coming from?", "Can you see what I am trying to tell you?" or "See it this way?" Similarly, if a person is a predominantly auditory person, the manipulator will speak to them using auditory metaphors like, "just hear me out once Tim" or "I hear you."

By mirroring their victim's body language and verbal linguistic patterns, NLP experts or NLPer manipulators attempt to accomplish a clear objective – building rapport. As discussed earlier, manipulators also try to accomplish this by sharing too much too soon or building early intimacy. The objective is the same – to strike a rapport with their victims, which then makes it easy for the victims to let down their guard.

Once the manipulator uses NLP to build rapport and let down the victim's guard through clever use of body language and verbal patterns, the victim becomes more open and suggestible. Fake social cues are fed to the victim to make their minds more malleable.

Once they build a rapport, NLPers will begin to lead the victim into increased interaction in a sublime manner. After having mirrored the victim and establishing in the victim's subconscious mind that they (the manipulator) is one among them (the victim), the manipulator increases his/her chances of getting the victim to do whatever the manipulator wants. They will subtly change their behavior and language to influence their victim's actions.

The techniques can include leading questions, sublime language patterns and a host of other NLP techniques to maneuver the person's mind wherever as they want. The victim, on the other hand, often doesn't realize what is happening. In their view, everything is occurring naturally/organically or according to their consent.

Of course, manipulators (however skilled) may not be able to use NLP to get people to behave in a manner that is completely out of character. However, it can be used to steer people's responses in the desired direction. For instance, you can't convince a fundamentally ethical and truthful person to act in a dishonest manner. However, you can use it to get a person to think in a specific direction or line of thought. Manipulators use NLP to engineer specific responses from a person.

NLP attempts to accomplish two ends, eliciting and anchoring. Eliciting occurs when NLPers use language and leading to draw their victims into an emotional state. Once the desires state is accomplished, the NLPer will then anchor the emotion with a specific physical clue- for example, tapping on their shoulder. This simply means that an NLPer can invoke the same emotion in you by tapping your shoulder.

For example, let us say the NLP manipulator makes you feel depressed or unworthy using language, leading and other NLP techniques. This is followed by tapping the back of your palms in a specific manner to create anchoring. Thus each time they want to create an emotion of being disillusioned, depressed and unworthiness in you, they will tap the back of your palm. It is nothing but conditioning you to feel in a certain way with linked physical clues.

Now that you have a fair idea of what NLP is or how manipulators can use it for submission, what can you do to guard yourself against NLP manipulators?

Here are some tips to prevent NLPers from pulling their remarkably smart yet sneaky tricks on you.

1. Be wary of people mirroring your body language. Agreed, you didn't know this until now but people imitating or copying your body language is one of the biggest red signals of them trying to manipulate, influence or persuade you to act in a desired manner. I really enjoy testing these NLP experts using subtle hand gestures and leg movements to gauge if they are indeed mirroring my body language to establish a rapport.

If they follow suit, that's my clue to flee! Experienced NLPers have mastered the art of subtle mirroring, which means you may not even realize they are imitating your actions. NLP beginners will instantly imitate the exact same movement in their eagerness to establish a feeling of oneness which is a good way for you to call out their bluff!

If you are looking for a way to manipulate people, mirroring can work wonders "Imitation is the best form of flattery." To make someone take to you instantly, be one of them or better just like them. Mirroring someone's words and behavior is a primordial instinct. It quickly makes people think that you are part of the "clan".

Have you seen how clever salesmen often repeat the words you do or imitate your gestures just to gently persuade you to buy from them? Or how influencers speak "the language of their people" just to win the trust/confidence of their followers. They are doing nothing but using the highly potent mirroring technique.

When you really want to influence people or get them to do what you want, closely observe their behavior, voice tone and pitch, mannerisms, body language, and speech patterns. Then, use the same in your interactions with them to make yourself instantly likeable. Works like magic!

Research has pointed to the direction that people who are mimicked are likelier to respond more positively to folks who mimic them. The way this works on a psychological level is that imitating someone's behavior pattern or words makes them feel a sense of validation. This positivity directly transmits to the person who validated them by mirroring their behavior. They come to associate people who mirror them as positive and likeable. Doesn't your self-esteem and confidence automatically rise when someone emulates you? And you invariably end up liking people who look up to you.

Another potent tip along the same lines is to paraphrase what people say and repeat it, which is also termed as reflective listening. This shows the other person that you've been listening to them, which sort of validates everything they said. Therapists and counselors generously use reflective listening (which is why people love to talk to them).

This technique can be applicable just about anywhere from your employees to your friends to your partner. When you listen to people intently and rephrase what they said as a question just to confirm that you are on the same page, you're making them feel more comfortable about interacting with you. They are likelier to develop positive feelings for you and listen to you more keenly because you've already demonstrated that what they say is important to you.

2. Confuse with eye movements. Another fantastic way to call an NLP manipulator's bluff is to notice if they are playing very close to your eyes or eye movements. NLP users often examine their target or victim's very carefully. The eye movements are scrutinized to gauge how you access and store information. In effect, they want to determine what parts of the brain you are utilizing to gather clues about your thoughts and feelings.

I say beat this by darting your eyes all around the place randomly. Move it upwards and downwards or from side to side in no clear pattern. You are throwing your NLP manipulator off the course. Make it appear natural. Their calibration will go down the wayside.

3. Beware of people's touch. Like we discussed earlier, one of the techniques NLPers use is anchoring. If you know a person practices NLP and you are in an especially heightened or intense emotional condition, do not allow them to touch you in any manner. Just throw them off the course by suddenly laughing hard or flying in a fit of rage. Basically, you are confusing them about the emotion they need to anchor. Even if they attempt to establish a physical clue to invoke certain emotions, they'll be left with a mixed bag of crazy laughter, rage and whatever else you did.

4. Watch out for permissive language. The typical language used by NLPers include "be relaxed", "relax and enjoy this" and other similar statements. Beware of this NLP hypnotist style language that induces you into a state of deep relaxation or trace to get you to think or act in a specific manner. Skilled or covert manipulators rarely command in a straightforward manner.

They will cleverly seek your permission to give you the impression that you are doing what they want you to do out of your own free will (one of their many sinister tricks). If you observe experienced hypnotists, they will never outright command you to do anything but seek your permission to make it appear as it is being done organically, with your consent.

5. Guard Against Gibberish

Watch out for mumbo jumbo that just doesn't make any logical sense or twisted/complicated statements that mean little. For example, "As you free the feeling the of being held by your thoughts you will find yourself in alignment with the voice of your success. Does this make any sense? NLP manipulators won't say anything purposeful but rather program your emotional state to lead it where they want to. One of the best ways to guard against this sort of hypnotism-NLP induced manipulation is to urge the manipulator to be more specific. Can you be clearer about this? Can you specific exactly what you meant by that? It won't just interrupt their cleverly set technique but also force the interaction into precise language, thus breaking the trance brought about through ambiguous words and phrases.

6. Don't quickly agree to anything. If you find yourself being compelled to make an instant decision about something important ad it feels like you are steered in a specific direction, escape the situation. Wait until a day to make a decision. Do not be swept or led into making a decision that you do not want to make on an impulse. Sales professionals are adept at manipulating buyers into purchasing something they don't oneed using sneaky manipulation and NLP tactics. When someone rushes you into a decision, it should be a warning signal to back off and hold on until you've thought more about the situation.

Chapter Four: Persuading and Influencing People

Gratitude is another huge influencer/influencer/role model quality. Efficient manipulators and influencers know the power of simple appreciation for channelizing people in the right direction. A simple gesture like thanking people, appreciating the effort they put into a project or publically praising their skills goes a long way in inspiring their loyalty towards you.

Always chose to recognize the work or efforts of others and focus on lifting them as glowing role models for others. Few things boost a person's morale than being presented as a sparkling example. This not just makes the person feel wonderful but also helps you reinforce what's the right thing to do. Everyone wants to be appreciated and valued, and will, therefore, be motivated to do things as they should be done. Once a person realizes that you are thankful for something, they will keep doing even more of it.

Another tip that can make you a superb manipulator, influencer and persuader is the ability to help people save face in a potentially embarrassing or awkward situation. The person will feel indebted to you for life. They will feel a deep sense of gratitude that you helped them out of a tricky situation, which in turn inspires unwavering loyalty.

You can help deflect focus from the person's blunder. For instance, if someone says something they shouldn't have said erroneously or accidentally, quickly change the topic before anyone notices or pretend nothing huge happened.

As an influencer or manipulator, you are showing people that you care enough for them to cover up for small embarrassments or misdemeanours. However, don't let people take advantage of your niceness. Ensure that the person is assertively informed in private (if it's a potentially huge deal) that you won't show similar lenience if it is a habitual offence.

Coach and mentor people instead of humiliating them. If you spot a sincere effort to change, help them change. Work together on strategies that can help them achieve their goals.

Be Relaxed
Relaxed, rational headed and steady demeanours are likelier to achieve success influencing people than emotional, volatile and demanding approach. Being level headed and unperturbed can win you more followers than an irrationally dogmatic attitude.
People tend to listen to you more effectively when you speak slowly in a calm, relaxed and self-assured manner. Launch into an angry rant of name-calling, and you're sure to lose respect over a period of time. Influencers seldom display extreme emotional reactions. They exude natural self-assuredness that ultimately helps them to influencer others about their ideas.
If you truly want people to listen to you, avoid issuing orders. It makes you come across as grossly high-handed and disrespectful. On the other hand, when you demonstrate that you truly care for others' inputs, people are likelier to respond to your request. They will feel belittled and do the exact opposite of what you ask them to.
Instead, make polite and respectful requests. Use the word "please" wherever you can. Instead of ordering a person to go on an outdoor sales call for the day, you can say something like, "Isn't it a lovely day outside today? Wouldn't it be a good

day to do your outdoor sales call? Slim chance the person will refuse. Request in a manner that people find tough to refuse.

Be Mindful of Your Body Language

Did you know that body language accounts for 55 percent of the communication process? And that the tone of your voice adds to about 38 percent of the entire communication? This simply means that non-verbal communication is more important than what you speak or verbal communication.

It isn't reduced to what you say but also how you say it or the manner in which you communicate something. Everything from your gestures to posture to expressions eyes impact the message you are trying to convey. For example, when a person has a stoic expression on their face and folds their arms across their chest, you know they are speaking to you in an accusatory manner. However, a more calm voice, uncrossed arms and legs, and a generally relaxed body language will make the other person feel more at ease. They are likely to less defensive and more receptive to the message.

Here are some tips for keeping your body language positive. Face a person while speaking to them. Maintain eye contact without staring and making the other person uncomfortable. It is alright to shift your gaze occasionally. Don't fidget or tap your fingers/feet. It may give your friend the impression that you are just not interested n what he or she is saying. One of the best tips to reveal your interest in the other person or what he or she is saying is to lean in the direction of the person. Keep your body language less rigid, and be relaxed or comfortable.

Body language is an integral component of your persona as a manipulator and influencer. Your voice tone, expressions, gestures, walk, posture and several other non verbal clues are a clincher when it comes to getting people to do what you want them to.

Always keep the tone of your voice assertive, firm, determined and low. Studies have revealed that talking to people in soothing and comforting low tones actually makes them more efficient. This is no way implies you shouldn't have a strong, assured and naturally confident voice that shows you mean business. Just do not go around talking in high tones all the time for the sake of asserting your authority if you want people to take you seriously. Always speak slowly and pause for effective to reinforce authority. You will appear less authoritative if you talk fast without peppering your speech with impactful pauses.

An influencer and manipulator's handshake is firm without being intimidating and tight. Your objective should be to assure people rather than establish a status quo with your handshake. Do not resort to a limp handshake by using only the finger tips of your hand. Use the entire hand. You get a single chance to create a powerful first impression, and your handshake can make an instant impact.

Did you know people seize you up and form an opinion about you in the initial 4 seconds of your first interaction with them? Make each second count. A firm handshake conveys confidence, affability, and positivity. It symbolizes the unison of two powers that can come together to create something formidable. Powerful influencers always shake hands in a manner that conveys their strength and control.

Do not use random, distracting or nervous gestures while addressing your group. Use gestures that complement verbal communication. For instance, if you are talking about a job well done or appreciation directed your company's way, use the thumbs-up gesture. These gestures support your speech and create a memorable impression in the minds of followers.

Always maintain a powerful posture. Strong influencers communicate confidence, self-assuredness, and strength very subtly through their posture. Keep your posture outstretched and open to project transparency, confidence, and power. Your head should be straight. Make unwavering eye contact while talking to people. Do not forget to smile.

One of the neatest tricks before presenting an idea (that you want the other person to agree to) is to practice postures in front of a mirror. You will invariably feel more confident and subconsciously convey to your audience that you are totally in control, positive about the organization's future and capable of setting powerful goals. When on stage, try to walk, pause and walk again for greater effect rather than making erratic movements or remaining stationary. Movement depicts energy, enthusiasm, and engagement, which can be highly contagious for followers.

Anxious gestures such as pulling at your shirt collar or lifting your hair indicates a bundle of nervous energy, which does little to assure followers in a crisis. Employees expect influencers to be calm and in control of the situation when they are rattled. If they detect nervousness in your body language, they tend to lose confidence too. Keep your body language calm, cool and collected to re-establish security. This comforts followers and facilitates collaboration.

Develop an impressive communication style

Everyone has their own preferences and communication styles when it comes to conveying their ideas, thoughts, and concepts. If you want to be in a more commanding position or want others to view you as an influencer, develop a unique communication style. What is your main communication medium? Do you emphasize more on verbal or non-verbal communication?

I once had a trainer tell me that she loved the way I used by hands gesticulate while delivering a presentation. It added more impact to the message and made it even more effective. From then on, I started consciously incorporating these power-packed hand gestures in my presentation to add more punch to it, which really worked for me. What is your communication USP? If you are wonderful with words, use it to your advantage. If you have a more expressive or animated face, communicate through expressions.

Find out your own unique communication preferences. I am an eye-roller so I can easily communicate through my eyes if I am not pleased with something. Take stock of your personal strengths, weaknesses and communication styles. You don't always have to tow other people's lines when it comes to communication. Stand in front of a mirror and observe your communication style. Pay attention to your gestures, voice, expressions, tone – how do you come across to the other person? What are the words and phrases you frequently use? Does your communication style encourage people to listen or switch off? Is your language positive or negative?

For example, if someone isn't performing up to your expectations, do you say "you suck at this" or "you have the potential to do much better than this?" Does your language bridge gaps or destroy relationships? Do your words encourage further conversation? Does it inspire your bosses, coworkers or subordinates to come up with ideas? Are you shutting people down by what you speak? All this is important when it comes to communication within the workplace.

People often have one of these three communication styles, which may vary depending on the situation. Some people have more authoritative or dictatorial styles of communication, while others are more submissive. The third is the assertive category, which is what you should aspire for. Dogmatic or dictatorial says, "I am always right. My word is gospel truth." Submissiveness says, "You are always right and I give in to everything you say.

However, assertiveness says, "I believe I am right but that doesn't mean I don't respect your opinion or your right to differ." Assertiveness is respect for yours as well as the other person's point of view. It is standing up for yourself without putting the other person down. It is the perfect middle way between being dogmatic and submissive. Look at the top management personnel of any organization. More often than not, you'll observe they have mastered the art of putting across their point without offending other people. Of course, they are plenty of exceptions too. I've had my share of bosses form hell! However, people who know to talk so others listen to them without getting offended have pretty much mastered the art of business communication.

Identify a solid common ground
When you find people switching off from a conversation or not responding favorably to what you are saying, switch to another topic. Find a common ground between you and the other person to establish a comfort level. People in sales use this communication technique all the time. They are trained in the art of building a rapport with potential customers.
Look for clues until you find some common ground. Engage the person in conversation on the topic for a while until they thaw. Make them comfortable, and then switch to the back to the initial topic. They'll be more receptive and open to what you are saying. We often give up when we realize that the other person isn't responding or reacting favorably to what we are saying. However, powerful communicators are quickly able to find a connection through a common thread and bring the other person to relate to them in a more positive manner.

Say Things At The Right Time
This is one of the most important pointers when it comes to communicating with people in a professional capacity. Sometimes, the issue in communication doesn't arise based on how something is being said; it is simply about when it is said. If you have an issue with someone at work, address it to them directly rather than letting the entire workplace know about it. Similarly, everyone has their bad days and moments. Show

more empathy towards people by understanding them. We all get stressed and have our share of unproductive or inefficient days. It is alright to reach out to people and make allowances for them when they are clearly having a bad time.

There shouldn't be any room for drama within a professional set-up. Ensure that you praise people publically when they've done something wonderful, and criticize them personally. I know a social media influencer who is extremely popular and loved within her community because she lavishly praises people publically. She always highlights their positives and publically acknowledges their strength.

However, when something doesn't go as planned or results aren't up to the mark, she'll call her staff inside the cabin and have a one to one with them. No one gets wind of the conversation she shares with her assistants. This makes her aura very positive and inspiring. It goes without saying that people take her word seriously and listen to her.

Similarly, keep your body language powerful and positive while communicating with people. For example, maintain eye contact to show that you are interested in or respect what they are saying. Be more aware and mindful of your body language while communicating with people. Imagine a co-worker is voicing his or her concerns to you and you place your chin on the hand while rolling your eyes periodically while listening to them. What signal are you sending them? That you don't care a lark about what they are saying or that you are thoroughly bored.

Always use language that resonates with your people. If you are dealing with a bunch of interns, avoid using too much technical jargon that they may not understand or identify with. They may identify with a slightly breezier and millennial lingo. Similarly, if you are addressing a bunch of senior management personnel, you may have to resort to a more technical and professional language that resonates with them.

Unnecessary technical jargon can complicate or confuse people. You may not be able to impart information effectively or convey your ideas in an impactful manner. Use language that triggers greater engagement and discussion. The main objective of communication should be to communicate your point of view in a compelling manner not to smart around.

Use the Sandwich Technique

The sandwich technique may not really qualify as a highly manipulative technique. However, it is effective because it helps you get the other person to do what you want by using the diplomacy card. This is one of the most powerful methods when it comes to communicating something tricky and potentially offensive to your partner. The way it works is – you sandwich a potentially negative or offensive statement between a couple of positive statements.

For example, "Listen, Bridget, I adore you a lot and you truly make me happy. However, I am having a tough time with you working round the clock. If you would just cut down on your work, and we could spend a good time together, I'd be really happy. It feels so wonderful when I am with you." See what we did there? We used a potential conflict causing accusation (you don't spend enough time with me because of your work) between two saccharine sweet sounding statements that are guaranteed to melt your partner's heart.

Don't throw a bomb on your partner by hurling accusations on them out of nowhere. Always use signposts or indicators that you are offering a heads-up about something so they are prepared for it rather than being thrown off guard. If you have genuine concerns that you want them to hear, begin the conversation with something like, "I really want to get this off my chest" or "I could do with some reassurance that..." This way your partner realizes that you aren't really accusing him or her but just need some reassurance and hearing.

Practice Active Listening

Again, communication is as much or more about listening than talking. It involves allowing your other half to know that you are 100% attentive and interested in what he or she is speaking.

It can be in the form of several verbal and non-verbal clues including eye contact, acknowledgement of what they are saying, paraphrasing what they said (to demonstrate you've been keenly listening and want to understand them correctly) and much more. Don't look at your phone or the newspaper while your partner is speaking. Let him or her know that you have their complete attention.

Resist the urge to interrupt your partner while he or she is speaking. Be focused, interested and attentive. I knew a friend who used to interrupt to offer his wife advice each time she aired her grievances at work. A lot of men do this, and it isn't really their fault.

They are simply wired to fix everything since primitive times. A woman may simply want to talk her heart out to feel lighter. She may not necessarily be looking for advice, guidance or suggestions. However, the man believes himself to be her knight in shining armor and starts offering immediate fix-it solutions. This can be true for women too at times. Resist the urge to offer solutions, and instead focus on listening to your partner.

After they are done speaking, you can figure out if they are soliciting advice. Don't jump the gun to throw in your two cents while they are still talking. Allow them to finish before offering advice.

Look at your partner while he or she is speaking and respond occasionally with a nod or verbal clues like "u-huh", "I see" and "hmm." Set aside a daily talk time that is reserved only for you and your partner. It can be during breakfast or dinner or just before you go to bed. Respect the other person's need for talking or even staying silent. At times, the person may not want to talk, which is also alright. They may engage in a conversation when they feel more ready or energetic for it. Even if you disagree with what he or she is saying, hang in for a while. Make honest and open communication your prime goal for a more rewarding and fulfilling relationship.

Pay Attention to the Overall Message
Reflect upon the message your partner conveyed via their words rather than simply catching a few words here and there. Check with them to know if you truly understand their feelings. You can do a check back like, "Honey, what I understand from what you are saying is" or "If I understand this correctly, then I think you are feeling…."

This tells your partner that you care about what they are saying, and are tuned in to their message. You are deeply invested in ensuring that you understand them correctly, and there's no scope for misunderstanding or miscommunication. Again, this helps you empathize with the other partner's perspective.

However much you detest it, meeting and interacting with strangers is an integral and inescapable part of your life. We come across people we know nothing about in our everyday life. The good news is – there are some smart tricks at hand to get strangers to like you immediately.

Here are my favorite tips when it comes to influencing and manipulating strangers.

Use Their Name Multiple Times
Strangers don't really expect you to use their names as soon as they introduce themselves to you or are introduced to you by a third person. Plus, people are naturally wired to adore the sweet sound of their names (narcissism pays). Once you get to know someone's name, use it a few times during the conversation naturally.

Don't overdo it or it'll come across as fake. I always notice when I address customer service representatives with their names a few times during the call, they become even more eager to help. The person invariably feels a sense of connection or friendliness towards you. The icy vibes of being strangers thaw a bit and he/she becomes more familiar when they address you by your name.

Also, when you repeat a person's name more than once, the chances of remembering it increases. This can save you the embarrassment of forgetting names (and permanently burying your chances of being liked by the person).

Smile and Maintain Eye Contact

This one's a no-brainer all the way. Smile a universal expression of linking or opening up to someone. Offer strangers a genuine and warm smile to increase feelings of familiarity. It makes you come across as more approachable, amicable and friendly. Plus, it establishes a more positive tone for future interactions. The tiny act of smiling leads the brain into releasing chemical hormones that make you feel happier as a person. This way, you'll enter into an interaction feeling friendlier, happier and more positive, which invariably makes you more likeable.

Eye contact is a universal expression or signals of confidence, transparency, honestly and genuineness. More than 50 percent of our communication happens visually. Thus looking into a person's eyes gives them an immediately familiarity boost. Want to come across as confident without bordering on creepy? Maintain a healthy 60:40 ratio.

Use the Head Tilt

The head title is a wonderful non-verbal way to communicate your interest in a stranger or to get a stranger to like you. You simply tilt your head on one side or another. This communicates subconsciously to the other person that you aren't a threat to them because you are exposing your carotid artery. It is the primary artery that supplies blood to your brain, and any damage to this artery can lead to instant death or permanent brain damage. By exposing this region of your body, you are signaling to the stranger that neither are they a threat to you nor are you a threat to them. You are non-verbally setting the stage for a non threatening relationship.

Use Empathetic Statements

Empathetic statements help retain the focus on another person, thus making you come across as more likeable. People generally like the focus to be on themselves and not others. They feel wonderful when they are the center of attention. Don't parrot their statements for it may come across as patronizing or condescending. Rephrase what they've said while keeping the focus on them. The standard formula for creating empathetic statements should be, "So, what you feel or are saying is ....."

This immediately makes them the focus of the conversation. Something like, "I understand how you are feeling." The idea is to always have the other person as the focus of your conversation. This basic formula seldom goes wrong when it comes to being liked by strangers.

Ask For Favors

I know this seems amusing and even counterintuitive. I mean if you asked someone for a favor and they did fulfill it, you'd like them, right? However, Ben Franklin noticed that each time he asked co-workers for a favor, they liked him more than when he didn't ask for favors. This can work for strangers too when it comes to breaking the ice and opening up people towards you. "Oh you work for XYZ Company, I was really hoping to get the contact details of the marketing manager for a brand association or tie-up. I'd be really nice if you could help me with their contact details."

When someone does a favor, they feel great about themselves, and if you ask a person for a favor you are helping them feel wonderful about themselves. This goes a long way in increasing your likeability quotient. It makes the person who is doing the favor bigger or focus of attention, which makes them feel good. However, don't overdo when it comes to asking people favors just so they like you more. Asking for too many favors will have people running in the opposite direction. Thus, you are manipulating a person into developing positive feelings about you by asking for favors.

Keep Your Body Language Open and Approachable
Did you know that strangers form an impression about you within the first four seconds of seeing or meeting you? The first four seconds are highly crucial when it comes to forming an impression of unknown people. This means the person will form an opinion about you even before you probably say anything at all! The onus in such cases is on your non-verbal signals or body language. Keep your body language relaxed and open.

Of course, actions speak louder than words. They work on a very subconscious and primordial level. Keep your gestures, posture, expressions, leg movements, etc. more approachable. This can help determine on a subconscious level whether strangers view you as an open and receptive person. Your body language will determine whether a person likes you or not, irrespective of what you say.

Keep your palms and arms open if you want to come across as a more approachable and receptive person. Your legs should be positioned wider, and the torso along with the head should point in the direction of the person you're communicating with. Added points for maintaining eye contact. Gesticulating involves using your hands to add more meaning or expression to your verbal message. For example, say pointing a finger in a bid to emphasize a single word or phrase.

This makes you more likeable to strangers because you come across as someone who is high on energy, expression, and enthusiasm. You come across as a more expressive, animated and articulate person. People respond more positively to people who are animated in their gestures.

Offer Sincere and Specific Compliments

One of my tips for breaking the ice with strangers is to pay them a genuine and specific compliment. It can be a tiny, casual and specific compliment that brightens up their day. I'd go a step further and ask them where they bought the stuff from. It is an amazing way to open up further conversation avenues. For example, you may ask a stranger or a person who you've just been introduced to where they got their lovely bag or wallet from.

To this, they may reply that they bought it from London while vacationing there. Bingo! This gives you the opportunity to talk about their English holiday. Thus, you trigger a happy memory, which makes them like you. Who doesn't love sincere compliments? A pro tip while offering compliments is to keep it specific so it sounds genuine.

Instead of telling someone how wonderful their outfit is, you can say the cut looks superb on them or you love the way the fit of the attire. Similarly, instead of telling someone that he/she is a good speaker, pick out bits and pieces from the conversation that you really enjoyed. Another favorite is, instead of saying, "you are beautiful" or "you have lovely eyes" say something like, "The color of your eyes is beautiful" or "you have a very soulful pair of eyes." Start with a warm smile, maintain eye contact, and then compliment them on their eyes. It works wonders!

Applaud them for the humor they used in the speech or their powerful vocabulary. Making the compliment specific makes you come across as more genuine than a plain flattery person. Compliments are a great way to get into the good books of strangers.

Make People Laugh

For all the communication tips I give people, this one probably tops the list when it comes to breaking the ice with strangers. People will adore you if you make them laugh. It is not secret that salespersons who make their potential customers laugh score high sales figures or customer service representatives who make customers laugh score high on customer satisfaction.

Ensure that you don't crack offensive jokes or resort to humor related to sensitive issues such as religion, rac, etc. Keep it clean, intelligent, simple and healthy. People are generally stressed, exhausted and bored with their daily grind. When you resort to humor, you lighten up their day by making them laugh. It gives them a break from a mundane existence, which makes you endearing to them. If they tell you they are having a tough day or were late for work today, give it a more light-hearted-spin. This will transform their sullen mood, and make them more receptive to a conversation.

Some of my favorite people in the world are those who make me laugh, and it isn't much different for the majority of people.

Avoid Getting Angry

There was a small boy with a rather foul temper. His dad handed him a bag of nails and asked him to hammer a nail into the fence each time the boy lost his cool. The first day saw 37 nails being drilled into the fence by the boy. Gradually, the number of nails drilled into the fence reduced. The boy discovered he it was easier to just hold back his anger than go through the entire process of drilling nails into the fence.

One day the little boy did not lose his temper even once. He went and told his father proudly. The father then asked him to remove a nail for each day he was successful in holding his temper. Several days passed and the nails were now all gone. The father then held his hand and took him to the fence. He said, "You did it, well son. However, look at the holes left behind. The fence can never be the same again. When you say things in a rage, they leave permanent scars behind. It doesn't matter how many times you feel or say sorry, the wound is forever."

It doesn't pay to be a modern day Adolf Hitler. Harsh reprimands may get people to perform out of fear in the short run. However, it will be least effective in the long run, owing to reduced team morale, low motivation, and a non-existent higher purpose for achieving the goal. Be patient and tolerant of people's weaknesses. Rather than getting angry, see how you can help them overcome these shortcomings to boost productivity.

The famous Machiavellian quote comes to mind. "And here comes the question whether it is better to be loved rather than feared or feared rather than loved." While a balance of both is ideal, love may help you gain fierce loyalty, companionship, and faith. It makes followers intrinsically motivated to put in their best to prevent letting their influencer down. This can be far more potent than physical rewards or reprimand.

You may believe fear is more potent and stable when it comes to getting tasks done. However, it can also lead to corruption and unscrupulous means in which people try to bend the system to avoid reprimand. Rather than acting with a sense of internal loyalty, they are simply doing things to avoid punishment or the wrath of their influencer, which may lead them to unethical means.

Take Adolf Hitler for instance. He was someone who led by nothing but fear. He rose to power quickly by instilling a sense of fear into his followers. People had little choice but to comply. What were the results? Devastating, to say the least.

Comfort People When They Make Mistakes and Build Trust

Always be a source of comfort for people when you want them to perform and intended action or think in a certain way.

People should be able to feel secure and comforted in the bleakest hours. Do not be a source of depression, negativity, misery, and disheartenment of your followers. How do you deal in situations where your spouse, employees, children, and others close to you disappoint you? Do you react immediately and cause even more damage to the already volatile situation? That may not be the best way to deal with the situation.
It helps to comfort people when they make mistakes or disappoint you because this only makes them regret the mistake than get defensive about it. If you launch on an offensive, be ready to accept a truckload of excuses and defenses. Rather than blaming people or accusing them, try to win their confidence by talking sense to them. Manipulators know how to forgive people or overlook their faults and later use this forgiveness as a leverage to build trust to get the other person to take the desired action or think in a certain way.
Let us consider an example. An otherwise brilliant employee Rick has been rather disappointing in his latest project. Instead of belittling him for slacking, try and comfort him to understand what really led to this unlikely situation. Ask Rick if there is something you can do to help him. Try and find out if anything has changed over the past few days or if his morale is low.
Accusing and reprimanding people may not take you too far. You may not reach the root of the problem. Fear doesn't foster constructive talks. Let us assume Rick has made a new bunch of friends, who drink in the local bar until late night everyday, which has led to him not being able to give sufficient time to work. He may not share it with you if he finds your approach condescending and critical. Once you identify the problem, you can work together to resolve it. However, to pin down the problem, you need to be approachable, assuring and comforting influencer.

Discard Grudges and Stay Positive

As a manipulator or influencer, it is critical to set the rhythm for a more inclusive organizational culture that thrives on progress, positivity, and forgiveness over back-biting, vengeance, and loose talk that can hinder productivity. Since influencers operate at the focal point of human relationships, every move of theirs should be directed towards setting an example for large heartedness and forgiveness.

Reflect and remind yourself that holding a grudge or ill feelings against people builds negativity within you and subconsciously helps the other person detect it. It soaks your energy and may lead to irrational or negative actions. It takes away the focus from productive goals. Walk in someone else's shoes. Imagine yourself in their place to try and understand what drove them to behave the way they did without harshly judging their actions. You do not have to endorse or whole heartedly agree with their actions. Try and see where they are coming from. Once you show people some unexpected understanding, they will feel indebted to you. This can be later exploited to get them to take the desired action.

Rather than holding grudges and seeking vengeance, talk to the person honestly about how you felt and get it over with. You will feel better and less prone to housing grudges after expressing yourself. Forgiving and forgetting the act needs closure. Do not speak to people in anger, while also freeing yourself from holding any grudges against them. Also, if doesn't help to simply speak politely to people on the face and hold grudges against them within you. Get rid of all ill feelings internally and externally. Show compassion, speak gently, try and understand what led people to behave the way they did and forgive them inside out.

One of the best strategies for discarding grudges is to come to some sort of understanding with a person or group of people. Get clear assurance that people will not repeat their actions.

This will gradually help you re-establish trust and eliminate grudges.

Forgiveness doesn't make you any less of an influencer. It doesn't imply that you are not operating from a power position or surrendering your dominant role. It simply means you are wise enough to let go of negative emotions and focus on positivity for increasing the organization's productivity.

Be positive is the blood group of all influencers. On a more serious note, everyone has some positive and negative characteristics. If you've found the perfect being, you probably exist on another planet. Great influencers, persuaders and manipulators know the value of cultivating a culture that encourages employee errors as a way for learning and growing. Though this sounds overtly optimistic, it leads to fewer errors in the long haul. Every failure can include some learning.

Rather than focusing on your employees' weaknesses, try and highlight their strengths even when referring to their mistakes. This gives a powerful positive twist to the process of evaluating their action. Let us consider an example. An employee Ann lacks time management skills due to which she missed a couple of deadlines. However, she is great with research.

Start by telling her how wonderfully well researched the project is and how much more appreciation it was capable of bagging had it been turned in on time. This doesn't make your team members feel devalued or de-motivated. They will be more driven and determined to learn from their mistake in the future. Simply highlighting the negatives makes the employee's morale hit rock bottom.

One solid tip for gaining people's undying loyalty and allegiance is to be good to them when they least expect it. People automatically assume harsh reactions from influencers when they make mistakes. However, if you treat them gently and compassionately by highlighting their positives, you are only boosting their morale for not repeating the mistake. Criticize or admonish the mistake not the person. A mature influencer does not resort to name calling and launching personal attacks. People get frustrated and demoralized when you criticize them rather than singling out their acts. It builds resentment and rebellion in followers. People will not be very comfortable openly discussing matters with an influencer who resorts to criticizing them over their acts. When people make mistakes, they are already feeling miserable about it. When you forgive them for it, they will always remember the favor. This gives you a solid foundation to get them to do what you want them to later.

Speaking harshly is like rubbing salt on their existing wounds. Do not say something like "you are such a terrible worker." Instead, try saying "what you did was not the best thing to do. Instead, you could have done this." This way you are still pointing out the mistake without coming across as personally offensive. Also, when errors happen and problems arise due to them, get rid of the blame game. Be a part of the solution instead of making people feel terrible about their mistakes. An effective influencer moves over from the problem and uses a solution oriented approach. Focus on how to remedy the problematic situation.

Chapter Five: Tackling Manipulation in Relationships

Emotional manipulation or being in a manipulative relationship is one of the most unfortunate things a person can experience. Not only does it destroy your sense of self-worth but also prevents you from enjoying fulfilling and rewarding relationships in the future. Manipulation goes against the ethos of a healthy, happy, positive and inspiring relationship.

While we are all in some way or the other manipulating our loved ones, it becomes sinister when it hits at a person's emotions or sense of self-worth for fulfilling a selfish agenda. Here are some effective deals for dealing with manipulation in relationships.

1. Closely observe your feelings after every interaction. Do a majority of your conversations or interactions with your partner make you feel confused, unworthy or overcome by self-doubt? By doing a routine check of your feelings, you will be able to identify a clear cause.

For example, if you realize that you always feel guilty after a conversation with your partner. Rewind to the conversation and go over what your partner said after each interaction. How did it start? What are the typical words and phrases they use while talking to you? Is there a pattern to what they say and how they make you feel?

It would be even better if you can make a note of your feelings to easily identify the emerging pattern.

Tell yourself that the problem is them and not you. Remember that you are only being hoodwinked into thinking it is your fault or you aren't good enough. The manipulator is most likely dealing with grave issues of their own, which they are incapable of handling effectively. This is only to help you establish a context for their acts, not to make you feel sympathetic towards them. Keep in mind, manipulators seldom deserve sympathy!

2. Assess your relationship objectively. If you can't determine if you are truly in a manipulative relationship or the person, get a reality check by talking to friends or people you trust. Ask them for an objective assessment of your relationship frankly. Do they think your partner has unreasonable expectations from you? Do they think your partner is taking advantage of you? Do they you are being emotionally vulnerable?

Sometimes by talking to a third person, we gain a perspective we hadn't considered before. It'll probably give you a new way of looking at things, which will allow you to act immediately if you are being manipulated.

3. Confront the manipulator. Consider various angles before going for the kill and confronting your manipulator. They most likely won't admit to their manipulative acts, especially if you sound unsure and nervous.

Rather than making blanket statements about how "they have been using you" or "taking advantage of you", get down to specifics. How does a specific action or words make you feel? List specific instances where you felt you were taken advantage of. Follow this up with a positive and gentle yet assertive request to mend their behavior.

You are communicating to the manipulator that you are aware of their tricks, which makes them more cautious while manipulating you. In the same vein, you are also giving them an opportunity to get their act together. It will take real effort and commitment on your part to move out of an emotionally manipulative relationship. You will have to stay vigilant and develop limitless reserves of self-esteem and positivity.

4. Hit hard at the center of their gravity. If nothing else seems to work, hit the manipulator hard on his/her center of gravity. They'll often resort to evil strategies such as befriending your

friends and then speaking evil about you or tempting you with a reward and then backing off or not honoring their commitment.

Since you know the person inside out, hit them where it hurts the most. Their center may be their friends, followers or anything they think is integral to their existence. Use this knowledge to beat them in their own game.

5. Don't fit in with their ideas. The key to avoid being manipulated is to reinvent yourself and have your own ideas about things rather than subscribing to theirs. Manipulators will shove their ideas down your throat since they need to control you to further their agenda. Have your own clear views, ideas, and opinions about various aspects of your life. Consistently drilling a particular idea in your mind is how they are able to successfully confine you in a box.

Don't try to fit in, focus on reinvention. Work hard towards standing out from the rest. Be different, unique and remarkable in your own way. Personal growth and building your self esteem is the key for fighting manipulation.

6. Don't compromise. Guilt is a powerful emotion leveraged by manipulators. They will use your self-doubt and guilt to their advantage. The agenda is to knock your sense of balance and instill a sense of uncertainty with you. This uncertainty eventually drives you to compromise on your values, ideals, and goals.

Avoid feeling guilty or compromising. Don't doubt yourself or your abilities. Even though you are in a relationship with a person, you don't owe them anything if you are not treated with respect. Every person deserves to feel wonderful and positive about themselves. If a person doesn't make you feel good about yourself or your accomplishments, there may be a problem. Have a firm belief in your values and ideals. Don't compromise on your values, beliefs, goals, and ideals. Remember, you deserve to feel great about yourself and your achievements. There should be a strong sense of self-belief, self-assuredness, and confidence in what you are doing.

A manipulator becomes powerless in the face of high self-confidence. They start losing their influence once you learn to operate with confidence and refuse to compromise on anything that undermines your self-respect or core values.

7. Don't seek permission. This is like handing the manipulator the pass to manipulate you as they wish. The trouble is, since childhood we've been conditioned to seek permission. As an infant, we seek permission to eat and sleep. All through school we are seeking permission to visit the bathroom, eat our lunch or drink water.

A direct consequence of this is, even as grown-ups, we don't stop seeking permission from people close to us. Instead of informing your partner you are planning to meet a friend over lunch, you'll subconsciously ask them if it is alright if you plan something with your friend. By constantly and habitually seeking permission, you are only giving control of your life to someone else, especially if he/she is a more manipulative type. Don't be overly concerned about being polite or making others feel good at the cost of your own comfort and happiness. Remember, you have the right to live your life exactly the way you want to. Emotional manipulation is about making you feel beholden or enslaved by some imaginary rule that exists only in the mind of the manipulator. They'll never want you to feel self-sufficient and take your own decisions because that diminishes their hold over you.

There's no need to bow to their authoritative dictates or consult them before everything you do unless it does impact them in an important manner. I happened to have a co-worker who would seek his girlfriend's permission even before going for a coffee break or out for lunch. It was ridiculous the way she treated him and tried to control every move of his. Predictably, the relationship ended on a sour note.

However, no one can make you feel miserable without your permission. And by constantly seeking permission, you are giving your partner permission to make you feel miserable – if that makes sense. You can disregard the manipulator's obsession with confining you anytime by living your life the way you to, without their interference or permission.

8. Be open to new opportunities. The manipulator wants you to put all your eggs in their basket so they can throw away the basket whenever they fancy. Don't lock yourself into them or be tied down by a commitment you aren't comfortable making. Don't be content or accept your current life. If you are in a highly manipulative or emotionally/physically abusive relationship, attempt to break free and explore other relationships or opportunities.

Manipulators in relationships often take advantage of the fact that their partner is "used to them", "addicted to them", "can't do without them" or "can't get anyone better." We often stay in abusive relationships because we believe that we don't deserve any better or won't get anyone better. There is a fear of loneliness or a false sense of being in the cocoon of a relationship.

Break free from such self-limiting and unhealthy thought patterns. Of course, you deserve better in life or will find someone who treats you with respect and dignity. To keep you your place, manipulators will resort to plenty of name calling. If you express a desire, they will make you feel like you are arrogant, selfish, proud, cold, and inhumane and many other uncharitable labels.

They want to keep you dependent on them. By seeking out new opportunities for jobs, relationships, hobbies, etc, you are only weakening their control over you. Seek out new people, make new friends, join a hobby club, volunteer with an NGO. Do something purposeful and meaningful that gives you the opportunity to meet new people and live a more intentional life. This is the only way to start becoming self-sufficient and independent.

9. Don't be a baby. If you are fooled once or twice, you are vulnerable but if you constantly let people walk over you without learning your lessons, you are a downright idiot. Stop letting manipulators take advantage of your gullibility. Develop self-awareness about manipulators and know how they operate. Have enough self-respect to refuse manipulators.

I know a lot of people who sleep walk through life, allow people to take advantage of them and then blame others for their situation. You can't go around oblivious to manipulators trying to use you to fulfill their agenda. Rather than blaming the evil around you, become smart and take control of your life. Yes, the unfortunate truth about life is negative and manipulative people exist. The take advantage of people to further their agenda

However, this shouldn't be your ticket to making the same mistakes again and again and crying foul. Manipulators cannot manipulate without the permission of their victims. Accept responsibility for your success and failure. If you are outsmarted or out strategized, it isn't someone else's fault. Learn from past mistakes. Watch out for a pattern that may reveal your own vulnerabilities. Don't keep trusting the wrong people again and again.

Similarly, don't keep giving a chronically manipulative person multiple chances. Break free from them. Remove manipulators from your life. Commit to the pursuit of surrounding yourself with positive, encouraging and like-minded folks who don't take advantage of you.

Remember, you have complete control over your life. Place your bets on yourself and not other people. If you place your bets on other people or rely excessively on other people for your happiness, you make yourself more vulnerable to manipulation.

Again, manipulation victims are not very confident about their judgments. Learn to trust your judgments and instincts. You know what is good for you much better than anyone else. Don't go around asking people things such as "What am I good at?", "what I do", "who is the real me" etc. You are simply opening the doors of manipulation. Don't go around demonstrating your lack of understanding about yourself. Again, I know a lot of people who go around seeking constant validation from others. They look at other people to define them. These people won't even buy a pair of trousers if it isn't approved by others. Why should others define you?

Define yourself and trust your judgment. Winners are not people who have a more evolved ability to listen to others. They are the ones who have developed the ability to tune in to their beliefs and judgments. They don't rely on external validation or approval of their beliefs. An established trust in your beliefs and judgments makes manipulators powerless. When you don't seek validation from others, they don't have an upper hand of how they make you think and feel. Start trusting your instinct and judgment!

10. Dependent manipulators. This is a little opposed to the stereotypical image of a manipulator but they exist. Contrary to most manipulators, a dependent manipulator will constantly make you feel like they are powerless and completely dependent on you. They accord you the higher position in a relationship to such as extent that you feel emotionally exhausted while dealing with them.

The way to handle this type of manipulation is to gradually get them to make decisions. Make them realize that they are as much responsible for their well-being as you are. Consciously put them into positions where they are forced to make a decision. Talk to them about how their lack of responsibility to decision making is stressful for you. Over time, they may enjoy taking responsibility.

Chapter Six: Manipulating Mass Opinion as a Public Speaker

If there's one thing that distinguishes influencers from average Joes, with everything else being the same (talent, knowledge, skills), it is the way influencers talk. Influencer talk is no magic language. However, it is everyday language spoken effectively. Influencers know the secrets of impact communication, and hence are able to draw a larger audience. If you've spent some time studying influencers, you'll realize there's something that sets them apart from typical employees. They exude an aura of confidence, an undisputed magnetism, and clarity in communicating their message. Their vocal presence is enough to inspire and encourage the crowds.

From Benjamin Franklin to Bill Clinton, good influencers are exceptional communicators who've mastered the fine art of influencing their audience through their voice and words.

They understand that their charisma lies in talking in a manner which inspires people to listen to them. So, what's "influencer speak," you ask? Here are some proven tips that can get you to talk the talk.

1. Ditch Those Verbal Clutches

People often make fabulous points when addressing a group of people, but ruin everything in an instant or lessen the impact/effectiveness of their points by including throwaway phrases that do not contribute towards making the message more power packed. For instance, people often end sentences with "and other things" "so on and so forth" and "you know things like that." These are nothing but lethargic linguistic slips that happen when you don't know how to end a sentence/argument with impact verbal posture.

These verbal crutches are most prominent when you take a pause while addressing a group or delivering a speech/presentation. The unintelligible sounds like "er", "um" and "aa" can be hugely awkward and ineffectual. So are gestures of lip-licking, dramatic hand movements, and constant coughing. These are all distracting or listeners, and seriously hit your credibility as a speaker. The primary issue is very few of us actually realize there's a problem in the first place.

One of the best ways to tackle this is to use a phone app and record yourself speaking on a random topic extemporaneously for a couple of minutes. Then, go back to the recording and note the number of times you've utilized verbal crutches. This simple technique will help you become less self conscious while speaking.

A good narrative and effective language involves using definitive words delivered with panache and humility. Refrain from using terms such as, "like" and "sort of." It isn't just weak and ineffectual but downright jarring for the audience.

2. Use Superlatives Sparingly

When you drop "awesome", "fantastic", "epic", "incredible" and the likes at every given instance, it starts to lose meaning. Over emphasis on superlatives washes its real meaning. Each time an influencer or role model assigns extraordinariness to commonplace things; he/she contributes towards making them sound repetitive, which means the really exceptional does not stand out.

So each time you're tempted to say that someone's presentation was amazing or the project was "awesomely" handled, take a few minutes to reflect on your choice of adjectives instead. Speak about how the project was well-researched, comprehensive and full of rare data. Generic praises or descriptions don't go a long way in inspiring people or getting them to listen to you. "This is very detailed and articulate" can go longer than "good work" in uplifting people's spirits, while making you come across as an effective communicator.

3. Resist from Pulling Back

Resist trying to equivocate when talking about crucial or tough topics. It is understandable that talking about not so pleasant things requires huge verbal and personal courage, however, there's no point in pulling your punches when important matters have to be conveyed to the team.

Resist the urge to use sluggish language since using clear, concise language will only boost your courage and help you connect/internalize what truly needs to be said, however unpleasant it may seem.

Use concrete and correct phrases to describe the situation. Clarify your stand if needed. As an influencer, you're going to have to learn to call a spade a spade. Practice speaking in front of the mirror if you get the jitters before a big or important presentation or address. You'll notice your gestures, expressions, body language and basically know exactly how effective you appear to an audience to make the required changes.

4. Simplify the Narrative

Use the age-old narrative for structuring your speech – Introduction, Body, and Conclusion. The less complicated your narrative, the easier it is to comprehend. Know exactly what information to include and what to eliminate to keep it brief yet impactful. No one likes to hear someone go over the same ideas repetitively. Ultimately, the thought loses its impact.

As a thumb rule, avoid speaking about more than a slide per minute, and more than four points per slide. If there's more information to be covered while you're addressing a group, talk only about the highlights, while you distribute hand-outs to your audience. Always attempt to open and close the presentation with a similar slide to maintain uniformity and a good symmetry. Use graphics and videos to aid your narrative and tell a good story.

Also, pay close attention to your inflection during the narrative. Too many aspiring influencers and influencers inflect up towards the end of their sentence, producing a highly annoying sing song effect that makes you sound ineffective and timid. Inflecting down makes you sound authoritative and certain, which is vital when it comes to influencing people.

The uptalk or rising inflection talk makes you come across as an individual who lacks discipline, confidence, and mindfulness. Stop right now if you're doing this.

Cliff hangers are another absolute no-no for a charismatic influencer. Many presenters reach a brilliant crescendo in their talks only to kill it all by not knowing how to conclude clearly and resolutely. This is especially true if you are influencing people to buy from you. You need to include a definitive "call to action" or trigger people in the right direction by ending the pitch persuasively. End with the required impact and a leave a few seconds for the audience to digest your closing remarks or questions.

5. Overlook Verbal Lapses

How many times have you observed presenters awkwardly disrupting the momentum of a speech by apologizing for a lapse no one even noticed? It's alright to stumble over a few terms here and there while addressing an audience or group. Unless it's a huge blunder with important ramifications, there's no need to stop midway for apologizing. Keep going as if it wasn't a big deal.

A majority of the folks don't notice these slip-ups until you voluntarily mention it, which draws pointless attention to it and takes the focus away from your main message. It doesn't just disconcert you but also throws the audience off gear.

6. Create Memorable Audience Moments

Most speakers mistakenly believe that the presentation or talk revolves around them. Nothing can be far from the truth. To make your talk more impactful, make it about your audience. They are likelier to listen to you and get influenced when they realize it is centred on them.

Recognize or appreciate an audience member, maybe a stalwart who has been working tirelessly for the organization and is due to retire soon. Hail a significant recent accomplishment by an audience member. The more you draw your audience into the limelight by recognizing their efforts, the greater are your chances of increasing your own recognition powers.

Chapter Seven: Manipulating with Small-Talk

Studies have it that when you meet a person for the first time, they judge you within the first 4 seconds of the interaction. Yes, that is correct. They decide whether they like you or not within 4 seconds of meeting you. Scary? How do you win people you've only just met? I've got a magic potion for that too – it's called small talk.

Though it may seem pointless, small talk is a brilliant ice breaker that pulls down elements of awkwardness and uneasiness between folks. It makes you come across as a friendly and likeable individual, apart from helping you develop a sound rapport with people and create a stellar first impression. Small talk also lays the base for a rewarding and gratifying relationship ahead. It creates a more positive and beneficial atmosphere that can trigger larger conversations. When it comes to breaking that initial awkward ice and setting the stage of a meaningful/fruitful relationship, few things work as miraculously as small talk. Whether it is a business networking meet or a dating club gathering, small talk goes a big way when it comes to manipulating and influencing people, building relationships and being a charismatic persuader.

Ever wondered how some people consistently manage to get people to buy their drinks at the bar or make friends in hordes wherever they go? Why do interactions with some people remain etched in our memory forever while we can barely recall others? The answer is well, small talk. Here are 15 rules for winning people using the power of small talk.

1. Stick to Safe Topics

When talking to people you've only just met, always stick to universal, harmless and non toxic topics (especially folks from another culture, place, race, religion, etc). Infallible small talk topics include weather, movies, world economy, breaking news, and food. A pro tip suggested by social psychologists is to base your conversation as much as possible on common grounds. Identify the common ground between you and the other person and stick to those subjects.

It is easy to gauge a person's comfort level about a particular topic through their body language (unless they read a ton of self-help books like you and have learnt to fake it). If their reaction to a specific topic is positive and enthusiastic, keep at it. Always watch out for the non-verbal clues when bringing up a new small-talk subject. Manipulators know exactly how to bring the other person in a more positive frame of mind to get them to do exactly what they want them to. Once a person develops a solid rapport with you and feels good in your company, he/she is likelier to do what you want them to.

2. Ask Open-Ended Questions

The golden rule for drawing people into a conversation or getting them to share more in your initial interactions is to ask more open ended questions. Influencers and influencers understand the importance of asking gentle and genuine questions that reveal that they are truly interested in knowing more about the other person.

One of the biggest manipulation strategies when it comes to establishing a rapport with strangers or making small-talk is gathering as much information about them as possible and leveraging this information to get them to take the intended action.

For example, if you've just learnt that the person you are conversing with is part of a local NGO, ask open ended questions related to it. What inspired them to be a part of the NGO? What are the drives that he/she has been a part of? Learn to notice what people are truly passionate about, and create a conversation flow based on asking open ended questions related to that topic to learn more about them. If someone's innately passionate about exploring different places and culture, ask about their latest vacation. Keep away from controversial and personal topics. The person will quickly take to you if you sound genuinely interested in knowing more about their interests.

3. Go Easy on the Humor

Sometimes people are so eager to make an impression by coming across as witty and humorous that they end up rubbing people the wrong way, especially folks whose tastes you know nothing about.

To avoid humor from backfiring, go easy on jibes, sarcastic remarks or tongue in cheek humor. It may seem funny to you, but the other person may not appreciate it. Even seemingly harmless comments convey the wrong impression about you. Intelligent/smart neutral jokes/comments are alright to a certain extent but don't make it personal.

Avoid trying to appear too clever or familiar by poking fun at folks without understanding if they are capable of taking it in the correct spirit. Take time to know and understand people well without acting all familiar and extra-friendly.

4. Disagree Amicably

To avoid making your initial conversation controversial, express your disagreement without diplomacy. Instead of launching into an acrimonious attack or defensive name-calling (absolute no-no), try a more politically correct (yet genuine) approach.

Say something genuine and non-controversial like, "that's an interestingly different perspective really. I am now curious about that point of view. Can you explain further?" you are stating that the view doesn't match yours without setting the stage for World War 3.

5. Be an Exceptional Listener

It's no secret. In a world where everywhere wants to talk about themselves, good listeners are highly revered. It is easy to influence people when they are convinced that you are genuinely interested in what they have to say.

People erroneously believe that being a good communicator is all about possessing top notch speaking skills. That's only one half of it folks. The other probably more important half is listening.

Being a social skills ninja doesn't mean you talk nineteen to the dozen without giving others an opportunity to speak. Influencers know when you let others speak, and respond in a positive/encouraging manner.

Show people, you are earnestly interested in what they are talking through verbal and non-verbal clues. Acknowledge or paraphrase what they say so they know you are actually listening to them. Nod, express with your eyes, lean forward and keep your arms/legs unfolded (to show you are open to listening to them) to reveal your interest in what they are talking through non verbal reactions.

Everyone loves affirmation signs that they are being eagerly listened to, which in turn encourages them to reciprocate when you speak. Exceptional influencers, role models and influencers understand the power of developing great listening skills to make themselves more likeable to their followers.

6. Reveal An Interesting Fact About Yourself

Okay, this doesn't mean you launch into a personal overdrive about who you are dating or that your bank account has just clocked a million dollars. However, a fun, harmless and interesting fact about yourself makes you instantly likeable to people. They will be likelier to tune in to what you say when they realize you trust them enough to share things about yourself. Don't make it too personal for comfort though – that's the golden rule.

It can be something along the lines of your favorite author and why you love his/her work. Why you chose a particular vocation or major in college? Why you enjoyed traveling to a particular place and enjoyed its vibe/culture? It should be like an interesting teaser of yourself (why you love cupcakes or why you decided to call your dog by a particular name) without sounding personal, boastful or over the top.

7. Avoid Conversation Dead Ends

There will be those awkward conversation gaps which you may not succeed in filling. The best thing to do in such a scenario is to look around you for clues to revive the conversation. It can be anything from a flyer to other people around you to details about the venue you're at. There are conversation clues almost everywhere that you can start building a stimulating and meaningful conversation on.

8. The Fine Question-Statement Balance

Maintain a fine balance between making statements and asking questions. A successful small talk brilliantly mixes questions and statements brilliantly to create more wholesome sharing.

Too many queries will make it seem like a one way interrogation. While too many statements will make it look like the talk is centered only on you, which can be highly annoying for the other person.

Role models know how to balance the conversation so people listen. Pepper statements with thought questions, such as, "I am really into aerobics and Zumba, how do you spend your leisure hours?" or "I really enjoy watching that reality show though most people think is scripted, do you watch it?

You're sharing your views but you are also giving the other person an opportunity to share his/her opinion. This back and forth technique gives you a nice, well-rounded conversation.

9. Empathize With People

Empathizing with people is one of the most sure-fire ways of winning their trust and getting them to like you. Don't confuse empathy with sympathy. Empathy is not about feeling sorry for someone or making them feel pitiable about themselves. It is about placing yourself in someone else's shoes and trying to understand how they feel or the emotions they go through. Saying things like, "I really understand why you feel the way you do" or "I truly understand how you feel about this topic" or "it must've been so tough for you but you've shown exemplary courage" goes a long way in building rapport with people. This sets the foundation for an equation based on empathy, comfort, and understanding, which is what influencers/role models need to inspire in their followers. People are likelier to talk and share their feelings with you when they realize you understand where they are coming from. Just don't be dramatic and pretend to weep crocodile tears in a bid to show you really feel for the other person. That's totally undoing it.

10. Keep it Positive

When meeting people for the first time, always keep the conversation centered on positive subjects. Even when you feel that the other person is threading on a negative or controversial terrain, gently draw them back into a more positive conversation territory. Also, stick to subjects which most people in the group have a decent knowledge of. You're obviously not going to find a lot of takers if you start talking about stock market dynamics in a meditation class or group. Keep it positive to earn the other person's trust before getting them to do what you want them to.

Before they take the intended action or 'buy' from you, they have to 'buy' your trust and faith. This requires keeping it positive in the beginning to build the trust factor.

Stay with topics which offer minimal scope for disagreement, conflicts, and controversies. Keep it balanced and simple for a successful starting point conversation. If you annoy the other person at the beginning with a bunch of negative or controversial topics, they are likely to switch off and develop negative feelings towards you, something you don't want.

11. Body Language Speaks Volumes

Body language or non-verbal clues can probably convey much more than words. Send the right body language signals to create a more favourable impression and make yourself more likeable.

Tiny gestures like smiling frequently, nodding enthusiastically, lightly brushing your arm against the other person, maintaining constant eye contact, giving out a firm handshake, maintaining an energetic/peppy tone and other similar signals can go a long way in establishing a more likeable and influential persona. Remember – you don't get a second chance to make a first impression. Let every gesture count.

12. Do a Little Digging

A little background work goes a long creating a stunning first impression. Whether you are headed to a party or an important business networking event, keep a few topics ready after researching the group's predominant interest. For example, if you find out that the host or business associate/associates are heavily into spiritualism or travelling or cooking, research trending/buzzing topics in those niches to start an interesting conversation. This will help you fit into the group more effortlessly.

You'll be able to make the conversation livelier and draw people out of their awkwardness. Scan the day's newspapers for prominent headlines, go through book reviews, read up movie reviews and ratings or learn about the newest health trend doing the rounds of social media. These good to know topics resonate with most people and can help you appear well-informed and worldly-wise in front of a new audience.

If you know the names of people you will be meeting beforehand, you can track their social footprints across various social networks (just don't go about stalking them and making it obvious that you are checking out their profile every 2 minutes). It is easy to gauge people's interests, attitude and views through their social media profiles. This will give you a good indication about their likes and pet peeves, which can then be utilized for a striking a gainful conversation.

13. Build on Similarities

This is especially true while interacting with people from varied cultures and backgrounds. Find connecting bridges and build on it at every available opportunity. Find a common interest, favourite cuisine, a book you both particularly enjoyed reading or some other nice common ground.

Even if it something seemingly cheesy like wearing the same shirt/dress or shoes, always mention it to set a likeliness platform. Humans instantly take to people who are similar to them. When people realize your tastes or preferences are pretty much like them, they will be likelier to listen to you or look up to you.

14. Don't Overlook the Grooming

While you may be excellent conversationalist with flawless body language, few things can create a negative first impression like careless grooming. Even though this sounds basic, a lot of people consider it insignificant and focus on the "bigger things."

Never attend any social gathering without showering or styling your hair neatly. Maintain goof hygiene and grooming. Use a pleasant yet non overpowering fragrance. Keep a few mints handy in your bag. Sport a neat hair style (that doesn't keep distracting you), keep your nails well-manicured and teeth - sparkly white.

Wear clean and ironed clothes. It is surprising how many lose out simply because they fail to pay heed to these elementary aspects. Clothes and grooming add to your persona even before you begin speaking. Chances are, if you turn up poorly groomed, people may not even give you a chance to speak to them. Disorganized and untidy looking folks seldom influence others or act as role models by creating a favourable first impression.

15. Ditch the Greeting Awkwardness

Greeting people when you are introduced to them for the first time can be naturally awkward, especially if they belong to a different culture or region. You may be stumped about the appropriate greeting. Some people aren't comfortable even with a slight peck on the cheek, while others may not appreciate a lingering handshake. In such a scenario, it is safe to wait for the other person to make the first move. If they don't, keep it universal – smile your pearliest white, say hi/hello and offer a brief yet firm handshake.

Bonus – Tips for Detecting and Outsmarting Manipulation and Building Your Self-Esteem

Like it or wince, the world is full of wolves in sheep's clothing. You can't do much about pathological and emotional manipulators who are out to leverage your feelings and emotions to satisfy their wants. However, you can beat them at their own game by using a bunch of outsmarting techniques. Manipulation, if not recognized and handled efficiently, can tear down your sense of self worth and sanity. By recognizing and coping with manipulation, you are standing up for yourself and not allowing sinister manipulator's to fulfill their agenda by tramping on your feelings.

Here are some smart and effective hacks for outsmarting manipulators in their own game.

1. Put the spotlight on them by posing probing queries. Manipulators are constantly demanding things or making offers from their victims. As a victim, you will be made to feel that you need to prove yourself all the time. You'll often go out of the way to fulfill these demands. Stop. Each time you find them coming up with an unreasonable request, shoot back a few probing questions and shift the focus on them.

For example, does this seem like a legitimate and reasonable request to you?

Do you think what you've asked from me is fair or ethical?

Do I have the right to refuse?

Are you requesting or demanding that I do this?

What do I gain from doing this?

Are you really expecting that I will do this?

Are you reasonably justified in expecting me to do this?

Who stands to gain the most from this?

Basically, you are questions that show them the mirror, where they can witness their real sinister ploy. If the manipulator is self-aware or realizes that you've seen through their motives, they will most likely withdraw the request.

Manipulators try to put the focus on you as if you are unworthy or 'bad' if you don't do something for them. You've got to put the focus back on them by making them think if their request is indeed justified or reasonable, thus making them come across as people with evil motives.

Questions will eventually force the manipulator to realize that you are seeing through their game. The onus of the action will now shift from you to them.

For example, if you refuse the manipulator's request, the onus of justifying your action isn't on you. By asking probing questions, you are asking the manipulator to justify the reasonability of your request. So instead of feeling guilty about refusing something, you are making the manipulator realize that he/she is at fault for having unreasonable expectations.

Also, let your manipulator know that you don't accept being treated they way they treat you. Make it sufficiently clear that you don't appreciate their ways.

For instance, if you are already preoccupied with something and the manipulator makes a request to do something for them say something to the effect that, "I do not appreciate it when I am already working on something and you make another request of me before finish the current task."

Similarly when a person is trying to force you into making a decision that benefits them say something like, "I am able to make my own decisions and would really appreciate if you don't coerce me into making a decision in a hurry." You are being assertive and telling off your manipulator without being rude. You are simply standing up for your right and informing them that you have the right to take your time to decide, and it could backfire if they pressurize you into making a decision.

2. Take your time in fulfilling a request. Not only will manipulators make unreasonable requests, but they will also

pressurize you into making a quick decision. They want to wield optimal control, influence, and pressure over you to get you to act in a specific way immediately. Manipulators realize that if you take more time, things may not go in their favor. Do the exact opposite of what they want by taking more time. Sales people are always focused on closing the deal soon. Distance yourself from the manipulator's persuasion and take time to arrive at a decision. You don't have to act right away however much the person tries to pressurize you.

Take control over the person and situation by saying something like, "I'd like more time to think about it" or "it is my right to take more time to think about a decision as important as this" or "I need to evaluate the pros and cons before I arrive at a decision."

You can use this time to negotiate in your favor.

3. Say no assertively yet diplomatically. This is an art which will only come with practice. You don't want to offend the manipulator by saying a straight no. Yet, you want to be firm and let them know you won't allow them to walk over you. Stand your ground, while still being polite and courteous. You don't have to feel guilty about your right to refuse an unreasonable request.

If you aren't up for something say, "I understand you want me to do this but I also feel I am not up for it right now. Another way to articulate your needs is, "what is the best thing for me to do right now is… One of the bets comebacks is to focus on your needs over those of the manipulator without guilt.

One of the sneakiest tricks used by manipulators is to make you feel guilty every time you don't comply with their request. When you stop feeling guilty about standing up for yourself or exercise your right to be treated with respect, manipulators become powerless.

4. Know your fundamental rights and worth. The most important weapon when you are dealing with manipulators is

to know when your rights are being violated. You have the absolute right to stand up for those rights and defend yourself. You have the fundamental right to be treated with respect and honor.

Again, you have the right to express your emotions, needs, and feelings. You have the right to establish your priorities, refuse something without feeling guilty, the right to protect yourself/love ones from harm, the right to acquire what you pay for, and the right to live a happy, healthy and fulfilling life. These are your boundaries and you can remind people to respect these rights. Psychological manipulators often want to take away your fundamental rights in a bid to exercise greater control over you. However, the power and authority to take charge of your life lies with you, and you shouldn't miss an opportunity to remind your manipulator that you alone are in control of your life. Distance yourself from people who do not respect these basic boundaries.

5. Maintain your distance. One of the most effective ways to spot a manipulator is by observing is they act differently with different folks or in diverse situations. Of course, we all come with some amount of social differential but if the person is habitually behaving out of character in extremes, he/she may be a master manipulator.

Think being unnaturally polite to one person and the next minute downright rudely to another or acting vulnerable one moment and then becoming aggressive within the next. When you witness this type of behavior, maintain your distance from the person. Avoid interacting with these people until absolutely necessary. You may end up inviting trouble. There are plenty of reasons people manipulate, and is very psychologically complex. Don't attempt to fix manipulators all the time. It isn't your duty to change them. Just save yourself by moving on.

6. Avoid blaming yourself or personalization. One of the smoothest tricks used by manipulators is to make their victims feel like it is always their (the victim's) fault. Irrespective of what the manipulator does or knows, they will never take accountability for their faults. They will always blame the victim for all their wrongs.

As a victim of manipulation, you need to stop personalizing. The problem is not with you since you are simply being made to feel that it's your fault so you giveaway your rights to the manipulator and become powerless.

Do not be led into thinking that you are a problem or the problem lies with you. I knew a friend who was constantly chided by her husband for working hard to support the family. He never missed an opportunity to remind her that she wasn't a good wife or mother because she was always working. In her mind, she was working hard to give her children a great future (which really didn't make her a bad mother).

However, in his attempt to gain absolute control over her, he constantly blamed her and made her feel incompetent as a wife and mother. Initially, my friend believed everything that was told to her about being a bad mother and wife. However, over a period of time, she realized she was simply being blamed because her husband couldn't come to terms with his own shortcomings.

Ask yourself these questions before blaming yourself –

Are you being treated with respect?

Are the person's demands reasonable?

Do I feel good about myself while interacting with this person?

These are important clues about the real problem.

7. Set consequences for manipulative behavior. Psychological and pathological manipulators will always insist on disregarding your rights. They rarely take no for answer, offer flying into a rage or becoming aggressive. Recognize and state

consequences clearly if they resort to aggression as a response to your refusal to comply with their unreasonable request.

An effectively communicated and asserted consequence can be used to pin down a manipulative person, and compel him/her to change their stand from violating your rights to respecting them. By reinforcing consequences, you are uncovering their hidden agendas and making them bring about a shift in their attitude towards you. Basically, you are strapping off their power.

It is important to stand up against the manipulator's bullying tactics. They will often try to scare you into giving in to their demands. Manipulators claim to hold on to your weaknesses to feel superior and powerful. If you stay passive and play along, they'll take greater advantage of you. Confront them and exercise your rights. Since manipulators are inherently cowardly, they'll retreat.

Research has proven that manipulative is closely linked to an abusive childhood or being victims of bullying. This in no way justifies the act of a bully. However, when you keep this in mind, you'll find healthier and more effective ways to respond to the manipulator.

8. Value yourself for who you are. Manipulators feed on the low self esteem of their victims. They'll always catch people who are vulnerable, unsure, low on confidence and don't know their real worth.

Rarely will the manipulator go after people with high self-esteem or sense of self-worth. If you can stay strong and take the manipulator head on by establishing your self-worth, it is evident you won't allow anyone to control you.

9. Silence is golden. Manipulators love drama. They will often provoke feelings of anger, fear, sadness and more in you to think they've scored points over you. The best way to deal with this is to stay calm and practice deep breathing. Concentrate

on your breath and how the body feels. Try to relax your muscles, and look the manipulator in their eye.

This simply body language of confidence and assertion can throw them off the tangent. A manipulator doesn't know how to deal with your calmness in such a situation. They are fully equipped to deal with your anger and fear. However, they don't expect you to react with calmness. It infuriates them and tells them the ploy doesn't seem to me effective on you. They will learn that emotions remain unchanged and shift to another target.

Don't get me wrong here. I am certainly not advocating giving up on a relationship at the first sign of manipulation. Manipulation can slowly pop up even in otherwise happy and fulfilling relationships, and it doesn't necessarily signify the end of a relationship. Before taking any drastic step, have a frank and open conversation with your partner or the person who is manipulating you. Gather the courage to ask them why they are doing this to you. These answers may give you vital clues into their state of mind and your next move.

If you've already attempted to have an open communication with your partner and they wouldn't have any of it, it may be time to explore other options such as therapy or counseling. However, you both have to be committed to the pursuit of overcoming manipulation within the relationship.

If nothing else works, you'll have to muster the courage to leave. I've seen people coming out of manipulative relationships through therapy, and they are not leading happier and more fulfilling lives. So it isn't like manipulation is the dead end for a relationship. If anything, use it as an opportunity to identify the flaws in your relationship mend these flaws gradually.

10. Practice self-care. Coping with a manipulation relationship can be intensely exhausting and stressful. Ensure you practice self-care to nurture your mind, body, and spirit, and don't let

the manipulation take its toll on you. It is common to feel stressed at the end of each interaction with a manipulator (been there done that).

When you feel your mental energy drained after communication with a manipulator, do meditation, yoga or deep breathing. It infuses a sense of calm into your being. Do something enjoyable and exciting to prevent the negative feelings from spoiling your day. Go for a long walk in the midst of nature or talk to someone you trust.

Solid Tips For Increasing Your Self-Esteem

The core of being manipulated is experiencing feelings of incompetency and unworthiness. Rarely will you see confident people with high self esteem and high sense of self-worth being manipulated. Psychological manipulators thrive of making people feel unworthy and imbalanced. By inducing this feeling of insufficiency in their victims, they attempt to gain greater power and control over the victims, and in turn use their sense of powerlessness to fulfill selfish agendas.

One of the best ways to immunize yourself from manipulation is to develop high self-esteem and self-confidence. By having a high sense of self-worth and positive opinion about yourself, you are preventing hungry manipulators from sabotaging you. Here are some powerful tips for increasing your overall self-esteem to make you less susceptible to manipulation.

1. Hold your inner critic. Yes, we all have that niggling inner frenemy who doesn't fail to remind us of how incapable we are at doing something or how miserable our life is compared to others. This inner voice shapes your thoughts and opinions about yourself.

Minimize your negative voice and consciously replace it with more positive and constructive terms. For instance, "I am so bad at this" can be replaced with "I may not be good at this but that shouldn't stop me learning everything I can about it and mastering it." You've just given a positive twist to a hopeless statement. Choose to use more hopeful, positive and inspiring words while speaking to yourself.

Stay stop loudly when you find your inner critic raring its monstrous head. You can also resort to a physical gesture like pinching yourself slowly or biting your lips each time you find your inner critic in hyper active mode.

2. Be more compassionate towards others people or treat them well. One of the best ways to raise your own self-esteem is to treat other people with greater compassion. When you make others feel good about themselves, you automatically feel great about yourself. When you treat people well, you inspire them to treat you well in return.

Practice kindness in your daily life by volunteering for a social cause (a huge self-esteem booster), hold the door for people, listen to someone vent out, let people pass through your lane while driving, buy coffee or treats for random people, encourage a person who is feeling deflated and similar other gestures. These will go a long way in building your self-esteem.

3. Try new things. People who are constantly trying new things or reinventing themselves are almost always high on self-esteem. They are constantly challenging themselves by stepping outside their comfort zones. They try their hand at everything and appreciate various experiences, which increase feelings of competency. \

When you keep learning new things and developing your skills, you feel wonderful about yourself. You avoid falling into a rut. Keep trying a new adventure or picking up a new skill periodically. Nudge yourself to be active, passionate and productive. Set your spirit and soul into motion every now and then by taking up a hobby, picking a new skill or reading an inspiring book.

4. Avoid comparisons. You are slowly destroying yourself by constantly comparing yourself or your life with others. There

is no victory in this, you'll always lose! It is a trap that will only make you feel more inadequate and unworthy.

Instead, look at where you were a few years ago and how far you've come to accomplish what you are today. Focus on your accomplishments and achievements today compared to a few years ago.

Albert Einstein famously said, "Everybody is a genius. But if you judge a fish by its ability to climb a tree, it will spend its whole life believing that it is stupid." Don't be that fish!

5. Spend time with positive people. Another great way to build your self-esteem is to surround yourself with people who support, encourage and inspire you. They should be people you look up to and should be able to influence you positively. It can be anyone from a professor to a mentor to a manager to a good friend.

Avoid interacting with people who focus on your flaws in try to bring to down on every available opportunity to feel superior about themselves. Look out for dream snatchers or people who laugh at your dreams or your ability to accomplish your goals. Self-esteem thrives in a positive environment in the midst of positive people. Be with people who make you feel good about yourself.

Also, be mindful of the books, websites and social media pages that you read. Let them charge your energy, not sap it. Don't read magazines that peddle unrealistic body images. Listen to podcasts that are naturally uplifting, empowering inspiring the next time you find yourself with some free time at hand. Watch television shows that uplift your spirit.

6. Sweat it out. Countless studies have established a high co-relation between exercise and healthy self-esteem. Exercise leads to enhanced mental and physical health, which in turn reduces stress and makes you feel good. It also brings more discipline into your life, which invariably increases self-esteem.

Exercise doesn't have to be boring. You can take up something fun and interesting like dance, cycling, swimming, aerobics, kickboxing and more. Anything that helps you sweat and gives you a small sense of accomplishment at the end. Physical activity boosts the secretion of endorphins within the brain, which makes us "feel good." And we all know how feeling good can have a positive effect on our self-perception and self-esteem.

7. Practice forgiveness. Is there some grudge that you've been holding for long? It may be related to an ex-partner, a family member during your growing up years, a friend who betrayed you or even yourself. Don't hold on to the feeling of bitterness. Overcome past feelings of shame, guilt, and regret, since holding on to it will only suck you further into the circle of negativity.

Conclusion

Thank you again for purchasing this book!

I hope it was able to help you to understand not just the ways through which people manipulate you but also powerful ways to manipulate people and immunize yourself against manipulation.

The next step is to simply use all the powerful strategies and techniques used in the book to understand manipulation techniques and prevent people from manipulating you in relationships, at work, and within your social circle. These manipulation strategies can be utilized effectively in our daily life to get people to do what we want them to.

There are plenty of practical tips, wisdom nuggets, and real life illustrations to help you gain a solid understanding of how manipulation works and how it can be used in your everyday life.

Lastly, if you enjoyed this book, then I'd like to ask you for a favor, would you be kind enough to leave a review for this book? It'd be greatly appreciated!

Thank you and good luck!

www.ingramcontent.com/pod-product-compliance
Lightning Source LLC
Chambersburg PA
CBHW070042040426
42333CB00041B/2038